High Vibe Eating

A Cookbook for Your Mind, Body, and Spirit

Kim Richardson

High Vibe Eating

A Cookbook for Your Mind, Body, and Spirit

Copyright © 2017 Kim Richardson

All rights reserved. No part of this publication may be reproduced, distributed, or transmitted in any form or by any means including photocopying, recording, or other electronic methods, without prior written permission of the publisher, except in the case of brief quotations embodied in the critical reviews and certain other noncommercial uses permitted by copyright law. (2)

For permission request, write to the publisher:

Kim.richardson@kimrichardson.kim

Available from amazon.com and other retail outlets
Available on Kindle and other devices

Front Cover Photo Credit: www.canva.com

Back Cover Photo Credit: Melissa Kim Corter
www.melissacorter.com

Cover Design: Kim Richardson

ISBN: 1979523835
ISBN-13: 978-1979523837

DEDICATION

Dedicated to my mother who inspired me to love cooking the way I do. Also, to all my angel friends who planted seeds along the way teaching me to change the way I eat.

FOREWORD 1

INTRODUCTION 9

SALAD DRESSINGS 40

RANCH 41

LOW FAT VEGAN RANCH DRESSING 42

FRENCH DRESSING 43

RASPBERRY VINAIGRETTE 44

ITALIAN DRESSING 45

ASIAN SWEET AND SPICY DRESSING 46

MEXICAN DRESSING 47

MAYONNAISE 48

SALADS 54

ASIAN SALAD 55

STRAWBERRY SPINACH SALAD 56

MEXICAN SALAD 57

CUCUMBER SALAD 58

TOMATO SALAD 59

COLESLAW 60

ASIAN COLESLAW 62

POTATO SALAD 63

MACARONI SALAD 64

ITALIAN PASTA SALAD 66

TABOULI 68

i

COWBOY CAVIAR 70

CRANBERRY CHICKEN SALAD 72

DIPS & SALSA 74

HUMMUS 75

SPINACH DIP 76

RANCH DIP 78

PICO SALSA 79

GUACAMOLE 80

APPETIZERS 82

BRUSCHETTA 83

SHRIMP CEVICHE 84

STUFFED MUSHROOMS 86

BLACKENED SHRIMP AVOCADO CUCUMBER BITES 89

VEGETABLE TORTILLA ROLL UPS 90

QUINOA 94

QUINOA WITH POTATOES 95

QUINOA VEGAN TACOS 96

THAI QUINOA 98

CAPRESE QUINOA SKILLET 100

MEXICAN QUINOA BOWLS 102

BREAKFAST 105

AMARETTO FRENCH TOAST BAKE 106

EGG BAKES 108

SMOOTHIES 110

BREADS 112

PUMPKIN BREAD 113

ZUCCHINI BREAD 114

LEMON BLUEBERRY ZUCCHINI BREAD 116

BLUEBERRY MUFFINS 118

BANANA BREAD 119

ORANGE CRANBERRY MUFFINS 120

SOUP 123

MINESTRONE SOUP 124

SAUSAGE POTATO SOUP...126

CREAMY CHICKEN AND WILD RICE................................128

CREAMY CHICKEN AND TORTELLINI SOUP 130

TORTILLA SOUP 132

GREEN CHILI POZOLE 134

MAIN DISHES..137

CHICKEN POT PIE 138

FLAT BREAD PIZZA 140

HONEY MUSTARD CHICKEN 141

PORTOBELLO MUSHROOM BURGERS 142

CILANTRO CHICKEN 144

CHICKEN AND MUSHROOMS 145

BEFF TACOS 146

iii

ENCHILADAS	146
FRENCH DIP SANDWICHES	152
CHICKEN LETTUCE WRAPS	154
VEGAN LETTUCE WRAPS	156
CHICKEN IN LEMON SAUCE	160
CAPRESE STUFFED PORTOBELLO MUSHROOMS	162
VEGGIE LASAGNA	164

DESSERTS ... 167

APPLE GALETTE`	168
NOT SO FRIED ICE CREAM	170
PINEAPPLE WHIP	171
DAIRY FREE CHOCOLATE MOUSSE	172
CHOCOLATE WHIP CREAM	173
NO CHURN LEMON ICE CREAM	175
STRAWBERRY LEMONADE CHEESECAKE	176
SPINACH ICE CREAM	179
STRAWBERRY SHORTCAKE KABOBS	180
STRAWBERRY SHORTCAKE BARS	182
NO BAKE CHOCOLATE TART	184
BROWNIES	186

High Vibe Eating

ACKNOWLEDGMENTS

I would like to thank Sunny Dawn Johnston who has helped me heal in many ways, who believed in me when I did not believe in myself. Thank you for empowering me to share my stories in an effort to aid in other's healing.

Foreword
By Paula Obeid

When Kim first shared with me her plans for this cookbook project and asked me to do the forward, I was super excited since I believe eating in a high vibrational way is for everyone; no matter what your size, your health, or if you are a vegan or carnivore. As with life, food is about making the best choices we are capable of in every moment and not judging our choice by practicing self-love and acceptance. I know for myself I've always been on the heavier side using food as an emotional shield. When I got closer to my 50s, I was starting to feel the physical effects of the extra weight on my body, so I started to look at how to feel more comfortable in my own skin. Some of this was working on the energy around why my body wanted hold onto this extra weight, but that is for another book. I also wanted to discover about how different foods affected my body and my emotions. So, I enrolled at Southwest Institute of Healing Arts in Arizona where I received my Holistic Nutrition Coaching certificate. My plan was not to do this as my profession but to support myself as I made the changes I was feeling guided to make in my life.

Concurrently, I was embarking on a wonderful spiritual journey and awakening to the world around me and how my food choices affected the environment, the animals and it put me in the low vibration of guilt. I was a beginning student of the Law of Attraction discovering how energy plays a part in my food choices and self-sabotage. I believe our thoughts create our reality which then translates to how we feel. I started to examine my energy including my childhood beliefs around food. I could start to see how the energy of my food choices would show up as life experiences. I could see how my thoughts and beliefs about food affected my body due to the mind body and spirit connection.

Many who have become aware of the mind body and spirit connection and have also started new self-care practices including things like yoga, meditation and starting to listen to our bodies. Specifically, tuning into how our body feels after we put certain foods into them. I believe listening to your body is the best starting point for a healthier happier you while practicing the art of self-care. Remember that being a loving presence in the world starts with you practicing more self-love. I have started to notice the spiritual connection that the foods we eat have with Mother Earth and the environment. I love that Kim has pulled together this beautiful cookbook for the mind body and spirit connection that helps us jointly raise the vibration of the planet by eating high vibrational foods. She has poured her love into compiling the recipes and helping to educate us all on making conscious decisions that the foods we eat can start a ripple effect of raising the vibration around the planet.

When I first started shifting to a high vibrational life, I was starting to not tolerate certain situations in my life and began setting boundaries with family, friends and co-workers. I also started to notice that my body didn't tolerate some foods in the same way such as wheat gluten, dairy, sugar, caffeine and alcohol. I understand that some of the intolerances were due to different ways food processed since I was younger. However, I do attribute some of the intolerance to my growing sensitivity and empathic capabilities. I started to listen to my body and make dietary changes including reducing my consumption of these items and foods containing them. I also noticed my sugar cravings didn't diminish so I tried to move away from processed sugary foods towards whole foods and fruit. Basically, I was gradually transitioning away from the Standard American Diet (SAD) to a more plant-based unrefined whole foods diet.

Many of you reading this book are also feeling guided to make similar changes in your life. It can be difficult but very worthwhile when you change the toxic environment in which you live including setting boundaries with relationships, making transitions in your career, or de-cluttering your homes and downsizing to a simpler life. Since you are reading this High Vibe Eating cookbook, I must assume you are feeling guided to make changes regarding your diet and move to higher vibrational foods. With the help of this cookbook, the shift to high vibrational foods can be easy with the delicious easy to follow recipes that will be loved by everyone you share them with. As I have grown wiser with age, I have discovered that it's not really about the foods I put into my body but more about the feelings and self-judgements in my mind concerning food. Over the years, I have taken simple steps that have me reaching for foods that feel better and leave me energized. I have gradually transitioned away from low vibrational foods that leave me tired and sluggish. In addition to being conscious about what foods I put into my body, I have tried to practice being mindful and grateful while I eat. I am especially mindful of not having judgmental thoughts and try to appreciate myself in the moment as a magnificent physical body connected to my mind and spirit.

Over the years, I have talked about the importance of trying to eat high vibrational food so that individuals feel better. However, the number one thing I share is when you're trying to change a lifestyle is to reach for highest vibrational foods that you can in the moment. Choose foods and recipes that allow yourself to practice self-love and nurture self-care. Please give yourself kudos for each positive change you make like adding one simple recipe from this cookbook since that is an act of self-care. Each act of self-care also affects other positive changes in your life. Since each act makes a difference on how you feel and changes the vibrational point of attraction in your life. High vibrational foods not only allow us to make changes in our body but also in how we feel. Remember how we feel allows us to attract other things that we want in our life. Every action we take that is more loving to ourselves then attracts more love into our lives. I was able to make changes in my food which affected my health and the way I feel in my body which allowed me to feel good as I move through this world.

"To become vegetarian is to step into the stream which leads to Nirvana" - Buddha

I am a believer in living a holistic lifestyle for myself

that includes primarily a plant-based diet that includes foods that are Seasonal, Organic, Unrefined and Local. Many of the spiritual teachers that I consider mentors are vegetarian/ vegan, but some are not. Since this is a core belief for myself, I am passionate and want to share it with others. However, no matter what your choice, please love yourself at every moment and drop any judgments. The worst thing you can do is to swallow a big spoonful of self-judgement and then use the spoon to beat yourself up. I am so delighted that this book introduces and supports individuals wanting to move towards their goals which may include more whole plant-based foods instead of highly refined and processed food that typically contain additive ingredients that are toxic. I love that this cookbook will educate and support you as you incorporate more vegetable and fruit produce, legumes, whole grains and plant-based protein into your meals.

When you start to move towards high vibrational eating, you might want to ask yourself the question "Does this food love me? ". Regardless of the answer make sure that you are listening to your inner voice and dropping any self-judgements. I think the best way to introduce friends and family to high vibrational foods is to share some of the flavorful tempting recipes found in this cookbook since it will dispel some of their misconceptions around healthy foods. This book allows us to move towards higher vibrational foods that can be found in the delicious recipes. Kim enables readers to move lovingly forward one recipe at a time. As Rome wasn't built in a day, our desires to incorporate high vibe eating into our lives doesn't have to be overnight. The Journey of Self-Love is a lifetime discovery of moving towards our truth. So please don't feed yourself judgment at the dinner table and select a recipe in this book that resonates with you. Please love yourself wherever you are on your personal journey.

From Kim's kitchen to yours these recipes reflect the love she's trying to put into the world one bite at a time!! Bon Appetite!!

Blessings and Much Love,
Paula

Paula Obeid is forever grateful to all the enlightened teachers that have existed throughout time and currently who have shared timeless wisdom to assist her on her soul journey of love. She pays it forward as Chief Inspiration Officer (CIO) at Bliss Always where she supports individuals as they recognize their perfection and that they are love. As a certified Hypnotherapist, Holistic, Nutritional and Life, Business and Spiritual coach. She works as an intuitive to help facilitate healing and achieving an individual's goals through a mind, body, and soul approach. Her passion is providing services, education and products that allow individuals to lovingly move through life with joy and ease. She can be reached at www.BLISSALWAYS.com where she provides coaching and holistic services.

Introduction

When I was a young girl, my mother was always cooking for everyone. She would take meals to people who could not cook for themselves and was always hosting the holidays. I have followed in her footsteps over the years. As I learn more about the way food is produced and processed and what it does to our bodies, I have made changes in my diet and the way that I cook. I love food and I am always thinking of new things to create. No Joke, food is always on my mind. When I finish eating I start thinking about when and what my next meal will be. Don't let me get hungry!

Years ago, I was a fast food junkie, drank Diet Coke every day and ice tea with artificial sweetener, I never ate any vegetables-yuck, and I drank lots of alcohol ... I was always the life of the party. My pantry was filled with canned, processed prepared foods for quick meals and junk food snacks. When I was younger, I was thin and never gained weight. However, as with all of us as, we age the weight comes easier and is harder to shed. During those years I would gain weight, then crash diet to get back, then gain weight again. I would make changes to my diet for a short time. Even with the changes, I would just trade out the "bad" food for "not so bad" food and eat way less of it. In retrospect, during that time, I was living in a low vibrational emotional state. You see, we all are vibrating on a certain level every day in life and sometimes we vibrate on different levels throughout the day. Low vibrational feelings include; feeling sluggish, anger, guilt, and shame … whereas higher vibrational feelings include; peace, love, and joy. Once we start raising our vibration, which can take a lot of healing work, we become more in tune with ourselves; our spirit, our body, and our mind. We become more present in each moment living in gratitude for all the little small things throughout the day.

It's easy to live in a low vibrational state and not even realize you are there. So how do you know where you are vibrating to? It's time to take a serious inventory; pay attention to your feelings, and how you feel emotionally and physically. Do you feel tired, angry, taken advantage of? Do you live in peace and joy EVERY day? If you answered no to living in joy EVERY day then you can always do things to work on raising your vibration. I realize we are all human and the life stuff can sometimes bring us down. However, once you start learning to vibe high you will be so protective of that space you will work hard at maintaining it. The most helpful thing I have learned for keeping my vibration up is having an awareness about your thoughts and feelings- all of them- all the time. I have total control of how I feel and react all the time. Really? Yes! Really! It was so liberating to discover that no one or no thing or event could MAKE me feel any certain way, that I get to choose how I feel.

The trickle effect of living in such a low vibration is astronomical. You are a mirror in this life; what you put out is what you get back. If you are vibrating low, you will not attract the high vibrational things in life. You see, when I was living in that state I attracted low vibrational people, friends, jobs, relationships, lack of abundance in my life. I thought the many people in my life at that time were my peeps/tribe and for that time they were. Although, I am grateful for the lessons that all these experiences and people brought to my life, as without them I would not be where I am today. I now am living a happy, joyous, abundant life filled with peace, love, and joy. I don't look back because I am not going that way! People come into your life for a reason, a season, or a lifetime. The people passing through your life will fit into one of these categories. Many come through to teach us valuable lessons. If we choose to not pay attention to the lesson, we will keep repeating the same lesson until we learn what it is we are supposed to. This was especially true for the men in my life. I kept attracting the same types of relationships and had the same types of issues. It wasn't until I learned that I was not loving myself that this started to change. Back to the mirror thing; we will attract what we put out in the world. How could I have possibly attracted a man to love me the way I needed when I was not loving myself in the way I needed?

We must remember when a door closes that it is for a reason and to not go back trying to open it again. This is true for the people we are in relationships with as well. We must trust there is a new door with something better waiting for us. How many times does a door/opportunity close on us and we think that we want it so badly that we keep trying to open that door? If that door opens again then we just re-live the same lesson all over again. It wasn't until I learned to trust that everything had a purpose which meant, the door closing had a purpose. That's when a shift happened. I then had to trust that a new door would open, something better and something new for me to learn. Every single time I put trust and less worry about the situation, something miraculous appeared. You see, worry and stress are low vibrational feelings. I often get asked, *how do you not worry and stress about things*? The answer really is quite simple. So simple in fact, that many do not believe it; you just CHOOSE to not feel that way. When you have trust you have faith- both of which are high vibrational feelings, the worry and stress go away.

As you raise your vibration, you will attract new higher vibe people and the lower vibrational people leave. You will be so protective of your little happy bubble that you have created that you will not let anyone, or anything compromise it. You learn to change your thoughts, set boundaries, love yourself unconditionally, and live in the present moment- not worrying about the past or the future. There are many pieces to the puzzle of learning to be in a higher vibration every day; Mind, Body, and Spirit. Food is just one element in taking care of our bodies. However, I feel it contributes to our mind and spirit too.

There was so much self-sabotage in my life, the nasty things I would tell myself or the ways I would allow others to compromise my happiness. One of the best tools I was given was the gift of loving myself-unconditionally. You see, I imagine a little girl living in my heart space. I sat and had a conversation with her about all the ways I let her down and how poorly I treated her. I vowed to never treat her that way again and to always protect her as if she was my own child. Now when I make decisions I base them on whether they are good for my little girl. Does she feel loved? Does she feel safe? If my mind wanders off and decides to say something negative to her like; you are so fat or you are a failure, I stop and immediately apologize to her and start telling her the things I would tell my own children when they are feeling down on themselves. *You are beautiful in every way, so you made a mistake, be easy on yourself and look at all you have learned.* I no longer put her in unsafe situations as I want nothing more than for her to feel loved, protected and safe always.

To keep my vibration high, there are things I have incorporated or eliminated from my life. Once all the pieces come together you have a beautiful high vibrational work of art.

- ✓ CREATE your day- does your day create you or do you create your day? I start of every morning with prayer, meditation, and setting my intentions for the day. I always ask, "How may I serve today?". I like to do yoga daily, however sometimes I may not create the time (notice how I said that?), I will at least do a few stretches to get moving. I always have a love fest with my dogs, we all get down on the floor and roll around and snuggle each other. I do this because it brings me joy and makes my heart happy … raising my vibration.
- ✓ Tune in and tune out – By practicing meditation daily and living in a higher vibrational state it is amazing how clear your intuition gets. I listen to

the messages sent from God, the angels, and my guides, whereas before I never heard them. Tune out the noise of the world. The very best thing I did was get rid of television service. No more news altering my emotions. Tune out the negativity on social media. Un-follow or un-friend those that post things that get your emotions going in a negative way.

- ✓ Do the things that bring you joy — Whatever that is for you, do it and do more of it! Take the time out for you and make sure you are feeding your soul. Play like a child, innocent and fun without a care in the world. Do small things throughout the day and do big things occasionally. Learn to say no when being asked to compromise your joy. I love playing music while singing and dancing around the house. I love having little kids around because my childlike nature can come out to play. I love getting massages every now and then and for my big thing … I HAVE to go Scuba diving as often as I can.

- ✓ Let go of judgement — This goes both ways; the fear of being judged and the act of judging others. Who cares what people think about you. You are living your life for YOU and no one else. I was trapped by this for so much of my life. I do not understand where it becomes a thought process that we are to live or act in a certain way and if we do not people will think less of us. Well, if there are people that think less of you for ANYTHING they are NOT your people! My dear friend, Sunny always says, *"Your opinion of me is none of my business."* This is one of my favorite sayings EVER! Realize that when someone has judgement around you that it usually has something to do with them. That brings me to not judging others. We have all done it even unintentionally. I had to start realizing when I made a judgement about someone else, what was that triggering inside of me?

- ✓ Heal from past pain – This is the most difficult part, but once you start this journey of healing your life will change in the most miraculous of ways. Take classes, attend workshops, or attend healing retreats to raise your vibration. There are so many resources available to us if we are willing to do the work. Learning to forgive those that have hurt you will change your life. If you are having physical ailments or disease then it is time to take an inventory, what's really bothering you?

> Disease means the body is in DIS-EASE. There is a reason the body is in DIS-EASE and many times it has to do with something emotional we are holding on to. If you want to live in a higher vibrational state, it's time to let that shit go!

- ✓ Eat in a high vibe way – What you eat and how you eat not only affects your body, but it affects your mind and spirit too. Start honoring your body by listening to how it feels. Our bodies tell us when something is wrong, physically and/or emotionally. Your vibe will rise because you will physically feel better. Get rid of the GUILT around the food, for goodness sake … if you want the damn cookie, eat it and enjoy it!

When you are truly loving what you eat and how you feel when you eat it, your vibration rises. When you can release emotional pain, you will let go of the emotional eating. The weight will start to come off not because you are eating healthier, but because you are healing your mind and feeding your spirit. During my healing process, I realized the reason I was eating the low vibrational food was because I was holding onto the weight as it provided me protection. I was sexually abused and taken advantage of by many men in my life. I held the extra weight as a way of not wanting to attract their attention.

Once I learned to set boundaries and love myself, the weight started coming off even before I changed my diet and with no exercise. I also changed my mind set that I wanted my body to look and feel a certain way for ME and no one else. Our mind plays an important role in all the issues of the body. It is time to get control and heal the wounds, so we can heal our bodies- not just the weight but all the aliments we have. Get rid of that stupid scale! I used to obsess over the scale, getting on it every day which lead to feelings of anger and shame. The best thing I ever did was throw that thing out. Once I stopped obsessing over the number and started focusing on how I felt, miraculous things started happening in all aspects of my life. It is hard to believe that the scale had so much power over so many things in my life. As I really paid attention to how I felt when I ate certain foods and listened to my body, I made changes so that I would feel better. I was stuck at a certain weight/size for quite a few years. Once I made these changes in how I ate, more weight started coming off. Now this took longer than any crash diet, so I learned to be gentle, kind, and loving to myself along the way. I would only get weighed at the Doctor's office, when they made me step on the scale. From my physical one year to the next I had only lost ten pounds, but I felt amazing. I loved how I looked and my clothes felt better. Instead of the "are you kidding me ... only ten pounds?" thought I would have had in the past, I felt empowered. I knew I was working towards a lifelong change.

I knew I had to work the mind, body, and spirit part of my vibration first before thinking about the food I was eating. Once I started healing and learning to love myself, I then started changing what I was putting into my body. I made small changes at first, starting with the Diet Coke. I never was a coffee drinker, but boy did I depend on the Diet Coke to wake me up in the morning and get me going. I never thought I could give that up. As the days went on, I created a new habit; having hot decaffeinated tea and started to love finding wonderful new flavors. Then, the artificial sweetener was cut out. Again, there was no way I thought I could drink my tea without it. Now even Stevia taste artificial to me. I used to have to have at least one glass of milk with my dinner every night. Now I don't even like the taste of milk. I eliminated the processed meats, such as hot dogs and lunch meat (even deli meat is processed). Just take baby steps one thing at a time and your taste buds adjust to where you won't even like it anymore. I was then plagued with high blood pressure and was put on medication. It was then I started looking at labels, mostly at the sodium content. My mind was blown away at how much sodium I was taking in daily.

With each label that I looked at I started really looking at the ingredients in my food and it was scary. All these chemicals that the FDA say are safe to eat; Trisodium Phosphate (paint thinner) in our cereals! Really? Butane in our spray oils? WHAT?

I started to search the internet for the ingredients and discovered horrible things. I decided if it had anything in it that I could not pronounce or identify and was not a part of a natural food group, I was not eating it! By the way, be careful of the wording they use to sell us their products- natural does not mean natural in the sense we think of it! Just like years ago the non-fat/fat free craze hit and then we learned those products were worse for us than the regular ones. For example, French fries should have 3 ingredients- potatoes, oil and salt … did you know McDonald's Fries have 19 ingredients? There are countless documentaries and information out there about how our food is grown, processed, and what it does to our bodies. So much of our food is genetically modified (GMO's) to make it look better, and last longer … what do you think that's doing to our bodies? Let me tell you, I once had a package of tomatoes in my fridge, I kid you not, for 3 months and they were still as firm as the day I bought them! That's just not natural.

There is the Gluten issue. Many people are developing

sensitivities to gluten because our wheat has been modified so much. They spray our food with pesticides of which the people tending those farms must wear Hazmat suits, and we are eating that food! One day I was checking out at the grocery store and the cashier made a comment about my more expensive organic apples, indicating the other ones were on sale. I just replied no thanks and she suggested I just "peel" the apple. Oh boy, don't get me started! It's not just the peel, it's the modified seeds and the pesticides that are absorbed into the food from the ground; inside and outside of the produce. They shoot the animals with hormones and antibiotics and feed them GMO corn, soy or wheat. My mother hit womanhood around sixteen, I was twelve, girls nowadays are starting to develop as early as eight or nine years old! I have to believe it's the hormones in our meat and dairy products.

There is a rise in diseases which creates a need for medications that put money in the pharmaceutical company's pockets. I believe that it's all tied to the food we are ingesting. I have had people say to me, "I have been eating this way my whole life and I am fine". My response, "Well, you haven't been eating this way your whole life because it wasn't modified back then." I also ask them, "How many medications are you taking? How are you feeling?" For several years I was really strapped financially so I never could afford organic non-processed foods, it seemed way out of reach. When I was faced with being on medication for the rest of my life and I knew one medication would lead to another, I recognized I had to make changes no matter what. Once I was no longer spending my grocery budget on all the processed foods, I created more money for the organic items. As I used up fridge and pantry staples (sugar/flour/spices and so on), I just replaced them with organic. Therefore, it did not hit my budget all at once. That lead me to looking at all the chemicals in my beauty and cleaning products too. I did the same thing there; used them up and replaced them with either home-made versions or more truly natural alternatives. I started looking for hormone and antibiotic free meats that have been fed with organic animal feed, which are not always easy to find. If you are eating meat, it's also important to consider what the animals are eating. It all comes to our body. Today, organic choices are more abundant and much less expensive than it they used to be. Bulk stores are now stocking tons of organic choices. Many times, I find the organic groceries on sale so it's cheaper than the non-organic. Be sure to check your local grocery store ads, go to their websites to look for coupons and see if they have apps for your phone. I have an app for one that knows what I buy and gives me discounts for those things even if it's not in the ad. As with everything in life, if you want it bad enough you can make it happen.

Now you may say, "I don't have time to eat healthy". I used to say the same thing. What I realized is that I just needed to think ahead by preparing my menu for the week and prepping some food on the weekend, so it was easier during the week. So now when I have the time, I create freezer meals that I could throw in the crock pot or heat up quickly during the times I was busy. Having some freezer options has saved me many times from being hungry and just reaching for the quick easy thing. I used to use instant potatoes all the time and now I buy a bag of organic potatoes and cook them up all up into mashed potatoes, place them in quart size freezer bags and when I am ready to eat them I just thaw them the day before and heat them on the stove. I have my own food prepared to be quick and easy. Sunday is usually my shopping day and when I use to wash, cut, and store all my veggies so they are ready to grab throughout the week. Now that I am in the habit of doing this, my weeks are so much easier. If I skip my food prep day, it feels hectic all week trying to figure out what to eat all the time.

The thing I have learned about food (just like in life), is that everyone has their own journey and it's not my job to control or change it. The other truth is, there is no right or wrong way. It's different for everyone. Some will say going Vegan is the only healthy way to go. What you eat and your beliefs are a personal choice. You need to do what's right for you. I always say … *you do you, bo!*

High vibrational eating is about preparing and eating your food with loving energy and intention in order to nourish your mind, body and spirit. I do not eat 100% organic all the time, but I try to. It's especially difficult when eating out. Just as you must pay attention to your thoughts, you have to pay attention to how you feel when you eat certain foods in order to raise your vibration. Personally, I can feel a difference eat clean. When I do decide to eat something processed or greasy, I pay for it all night long and am sluggish for days. Some foods I make have sugar or other things people consider "bad". If you feel like it's bad and you have guilt around it as you are eating it, then it's entering your body in a lower vibrational state. If you want that decadent chocolate cake, then have it. Create it with love and enjoy it. Savor it while only eating what feels good to you. However, if you wind up eating the entire cake and feel sick afterwards, eating to stuff your emotions, or feel guilty, then that is low vibrational eating. I genuinely have a love for all the food I create and ingest … that is high vibrational eating. Have fun creating your food, infuse it with love and enjoy every bite you take. This book isn't about a diet. It's about a new perspective around food and creating a new way of life.

You may have heard of The Paleo Approach or The Whole 30 Diet ... both are about clean eating. The premise of the Whole 30 cookbook is eliminating the processed foods, chemicals, and foods that often cause body inflammation issues like gluten and dairy for 30 days. Then, slowly one by one introduce it back into your body to see how your body reacts to it. They are both inspirational books for lots of non-processed recipes.

You can find great recipes online these days. Pinterest is my favorite go to place for inspiration. I always use recipes as inspiration and modify them to my personal liking and I encourage you to do the same. If it's something completely new, then I will usually follow the recipe exactly. I can then decide how I may want to modify it for next time. Please be sure to modify my recipes to your liking. I hope you find some inspiration in some of the recipes I am going to share with you. Enjoy creating your food with loving intentions.

Now let me explain the way I cook. I really do not measure anything. I like to just toss things together like an artist creating something beautiful. Therefore, the measurements are an approximation. You will want to adjust them to your liking. Not all the recipes in this book are sugar-free or dairy-free. The recipes in this book are some of my favorite dishes that I love to create. People always enjoy them which is high vibrational eating.

The ingredients will be listed. Know that most of the time I use all organic or at least non-GMO ingredients. However, it won't be stated in each ingredient as that is your personal choice. There are suggestions on how you can change up the recipe to fit your personal needs. For example, if it calls for milk you can substitute almond milk or any other non-dairy milk product. Remember to do what works for you. The key is how you are feeling when you prepare it and eat it.

You will notice on each page there is room for you to make some notes about the recipe- what you changed or would like to change for next time. I do not know how many times I make something and decide I tweak the recipe and when I go back to it I can't remember the changes I was planning.

Sending you love on your high vibrational journey!

Getting Prepared

For your meal prepping to be less stressful, it is important to understand that having the right things stocked in your kitchen and the right tools to prepare your meals makes a huge difference. I will share with you what items/tools I always have on hand to make my life easier in the kitchen.

Pantry Items

To be able to create beautiful things in the kitchen, you will want a well-stocked pantry with a variety spices and staples. You do not have to go buy everything all at once. Just pick up one or two items every time you go to the store so it's not such a huge impact on your budget all at once. Then when you run out of something, replace it right away so your pantry is always stocked. It's a lot less stressful when you are planning a meal not to have to buy 5 staple items in addition to the other ingredients all at once. Even though organic, or at least non-GMO versions fit my beliefs, you can do what feels right for you. Here are some basic pantry items I always have on hand.

Staples

- ☐ Cornstarch
- ☐ Flour- there are lots of flour alternatives available these days if you have a gluten sensitivity
- ☐ Sugar
- ☐ Brown Sugar
- ☐ Honey/Agave
- ☐ Peanut butter
- ☐ Apple Sauce
- ☐ Vanilla
- ☐ Quinoa
- ☐ Sesame Oil
- ☐ Oil- I mostly use extra virgin olive oil
- ☐ Light olive oil just for making mayonnaise
- ☐ Non-stick cooking spray, no butane!

Vinegars/Sauces

- ☐ Red Wine Vinegar
- ☐ Rice Wine Vinegar
- ☐ Balsamic Vinegar
- ☐ Worchester sauce
- ☐ Chili paste

☐ Chinese hot mustard

Canned Goods

I really do not use many canned items anymore. Many are packed with preservatives and are loaded with sodium.

☐ Diced tomatoes
☐ Tomato Sauce
☐ Chicken and/or Vegetable broth
☐ Garbanzo beans/or other favorite beans

Dried Pasta

You choose your favorites. I love edamame pasta, but I usually have a few varieties on hand. I enjoy buying special shaped pasta like hearts and peace signs, it just feels good serving all that love. I mostly find the fun shaped pastas online. It's just important that you have a variety of pastas in your pantry so you can make any recipe quickly. I am so happy to see grocers carrying a larger variety of organic, gluten free pastas as well.

Dried Spices

I like to find organic spices and create my own spice mixes so that I can have control over the sodium content as well as the ingredients. Many store-bought combined spices have chemical binders in them. You will notice I do not use salt in many of my recipes, especially ones calling for cheese or bacon as they already contain a high amount of sodium. I am watching my sodium and I figure people can add it if they want it. I have not missed it at all.

- ☐ Salt/Pepper – I like fresh ground Himalayan Pink Sea Salt and Fresh Peppercorns
- ☐ Garlic Powder (I use a special garlic seasoning in place of garlic powder)
- ☐ Basil
- ☐ Oregano
- ☐ Thyme
- ☐ Rosemary
- ☐ Cocoa Powder
- ☐ Cinnamon
- ☐ Cumin
- ☐ Chili Powder
- ☐ Red Cayenne Pepper
- ☐ Red Pepper Flakes
- ☐ Ground Mustard
- ☐ Bay Leaves
- ☐ Ground Ginger

Fresh Herbs

I always have organic fresh herbs on hand at all times. I have quite the collection of plants in my house. I plan on doing a full organic garden outside soon. However, since it snows here in the winter, I keep lots of herbs in the house. My favorites are basil (lots of basil!), oregano, and mint. I do use cilantro and parsley a lot in my recipes, however I have not been good at growing those myself. If you are not interested in growing your own, then you can purchase them fresh at the store when you plan on using them. Fresh herbs bring wonderful life to all your creations.

Tools

As with any job, having the right tools makes a huge difference on the ease of the job. There are many kitchen gadgets that make preparing your meals easier. Some are a little expensive. It took me a lot of years to collect all my gadgets and I love having them so much! Take good care of them and they will last you forever.

Must Have Tools:

Pots and Pans- these are a personal preference for everyone. Some like non-stick and some like stainless. I have a set of pans that are 10 years old and still look brand new because they are well taken care of. To take care of your pans; do not cook with high heat, do not rinse to cool off (let them cool naturally), use the right utensils so you do not scratch them, and be protective of them ... I never let anyone cook with my good pans in my kitchen.

A few good knives- keep them sharp. Do not use your knives for anything other than cutting food. I love my Cutco knives and have had them for over 20 years now. I mostly use my French chef, small thin boning, and paring knives. I have a couple of good serrated edged ones as well.

A nice set of mixing bowls- I like the metal ones because they are light-weight and store easily.

A coffee grinder- designated for spices. To speed things up in the kitchen I will often grind my pepper right before a catering event.

A food processor- with cheese shredding attachment. I no longer buy pre-shredded cheese because it's coated with chemical powder to preserve and keep the cheese separated. I use my food processor all the time to chop everything to make meal prepping quicker.

A good blender- I have a BlendTec, however Vitamix is another great brand. This is great for sauces, soups, smoothies, and dressings. These blenders have the power to grind up an avocado seed (which is loaded with nutrients by the way) in your smoothies. They will emulsify anything. I really don't like smoothies with chunks of anything, this blender works well for me.

An immersion hand blender- I purchased the one with the extra attachments and little chopper and it's very handy. I mostly use this to make mayonnaise and pesto, however this is great for blending soups and sauces to

A good spiralizer- I used to have a small hand one and man, was it time consuming and tiring to make enough zoodles (zucchini or squash noodles) for a meal. Spend the money on a good hand crank one. You will thank me later.

Salad Spinner- You can wash your leafy greens and herbs then spin the water out right away. I used to lay all my lettuce out on a towel to try to get some of the water off because nobody wants wet lettuce. It would take forever, and I had to prepare it well in advance. Not now, thanks to my salad spinner. I have had several and my favorite one is collapsible, so it stores and travels easily for my catering events.

Now if you are a baker, a KitchenAid mixer is another great kitchen tool. I am just starting to bake more so I haven't really needed one until now. I do not have one, but can you guess what my next gadget will be? I am mostly excited about this mixer, so I can start making my own homemade pasta. If you do not have a KitchenAid mixer, just make sure you have a hand held electric mixer. That is what I have had and used my whole life and it works great. The kitchen aid mixer just provides a hands-free option to make things a bit easier.

You don't have to have all these gadgets. They just really make life easier in the kitchen. If you were to get one gadget listed above, I would suggest the Immersion blender with the chopping attachment because it would be the most versatile one.

Food Safety

Always keep your meat preparation area and the tools used separated. Wash your hands often and especially after handling meat! I usually use paper plates to cut meat. I can throw them away and not worry about cross contamination on my cutting boards. I use paper towels as a rag to wash my tools prior to sanitizing them to ensure there is not meat bacteria on my kitchen washcloths or towels. I have put cooked chicken in my food processor but never raw. Many people do, however just be sure if you do that you really wash and sanitize all the pieces of your processor after. I wash and sanitize my sink and tools well before doing anything. I often wear gloves when handling meat just to make sure nothing gets under my nails which can be hard to clean well. Be mindful of handling meat and then handling other things like seasonings. I try to keep one hand free of raw meat, so I can use my seasonings without cross contamination.

Be sure to wash all your produce well before using, even pre-packaged ones. Do not use the same cutting boards or knives that you used to prep your meat or prep your raw veggies next to your meat prep area!

Keep things at the right temperatures; keep hot food warm and cold food cold until ready for use. Always thaw meat in the fridge to make sure bacteria doesn't start growing and be sure to cook foods to the proper temperatures. Use a thermometer! You can find meat cooking guidelines on the internet.

Food Substitutes

If you have a sensitivity to certain foods like dairy or gluten, here are some easy substitutions. Just use the substitute in the same amount for any recipe.

Dairy- Use any non-dairy milk like almond milk. For cheese or sour cream, there are many dairy free options available these days. For butter, you can use dairy-free or substitute olive oil.

Flour- Use a flour substitute like almond flour or coconut flour. There is gluten free all-purpose baking flour readily as well.

Bread or Bread Crumbs- you can use gluten free for both.

Chicken Broth- If you are vegan, use vegetable broth instead.

Meat- If you are vegetarian and the recipe looks good to you but has meat, just omit the meat. It will still be delicious.

Just Get to Cooking!

Whatever the energy you have as you are preparing your meal is the energy that you and others will absorb as it is eaten. I know when I have been vibing low and I get in the kitchen, my food never tastes as good. Something just isn't right. Get rid of the feelings of fear you might have that it might not turn out right, so what? I have made plenty of meals that did not work out. We just reach for some leftovers, order pizza, or decide to go out to eat. No big deal! If you do not feel like cooking one day, then don't. Trust me when I tell you your family will find something to eat. If you plan and prepare ahead of time, it will make your life easier and you will stress less about cooking.

Use leftovers! For example, I will often cook a roast or chicken breast in the crockpot on Sunday and use the meat for a variety of dishes throughout the week. Don't be afraid of getting creative. I love re-inventing leftovers! I used to throw just about all leftovers in the garbage, whereas now I save them and base my meal planning on what needs to get used up. You will not only save a ton of money eating leftovers for lunch rather than going out every day, but you will have healthier alternatives when you take the time to meal plan and prep.

You do not have to plan every meal to be a five-course meal. Most of my meals are a main dish (often a one-dish meal) and a side such as a vegetable. I save the more elaborate stuff like desserts for special occasions. When preparing a large meal for guests, such as a party or Thanksgiving, I try to prepare as much as I can ahead of time so that I can spend time with my guests and not in the kitchen. Most desserts can be made ahead of time and for the things I need to throw together right before cooking, I will at least chop all the veggies the day before so that time consuming part is out of the way. Also, do not forget about your crock-pot! It's not only great for cooking but keeping things warm until guests arrive. I love using my crock-pot for soups, mashed potatoes, roasts, one-pot meals, and shredded chicken.

SALAD DRESSINGS

Store bought dressings are loaded with chemicals, sugar, and preservatives. I love having fresh healthy dressing for my salads which I eat most every day. Eating salads every day can get boring, so by changing up the dressings and salad toppings it keeps it interesting. These dressings are fresh with no preservatives so be sure to store them in the fridge (I like to pull the oil dressings out about an hour before serving) for no longer than 1 week. I have little dressing bottles with drip top lids that work well, but you can use any airtight container like a mason jar. Be sure to give them a good shake prior to serving.

Ranch

Ingredients:

1 clove (to 2 cloves) garlic

Salt/Pepper to taste

¼ cup Italian flat-leaf parsley

2 tablespoons fresh chives

1 cup mayonnaise

½ cup sour cream

Buttermilk (as needed to desired consistency)

White vinegar (optional, to taste)

Worcestershire sauce (optional, to taste)

Fresh dill (optional, to taste)

Paprika (optional, to taste)

Fresh oregano (optional, to taste)

Directions:

Add all ingredients except chopped chives and buttermilk into the blender. Blend until smooth, gradually add your buttermilk until you reach desired consistency. Sprinkle in the chives and mix well with a spatula. Store in the fridge until ready to serve. You can use vegan sour cream, mayo, and use almond milk if desired. It will be a little bit thinner but still delicious

Low Fat Vegan Ranch Dressing

Ingredients:

1 avocado

1 teaspoon dried dill

1 clove garlic, peeled

1 teaspoon garlic powder

2 tablespoons fresh chopped parsley

2 tablespoons fresh chopped chives

2 tablespoons lemon juice

¼ cup olive oil

½ cup almond milk

Salt and pepper to taste

Directions:

Add all ingredients except chopped chives and Almond Milk into the blender. If you have a good blender like a Blendtec or Vitamix you can even place the avocado seed in the blender, it has so many great nutrients. Do NOT try that with a regular blender you may break it. Blend until smooth, gradually add your Almond Milk until you reach desired consistency. Sprinkle in the chives and mix. Store in the fridge until ready to serve. It will turn brown quickly, I always recommend when storing in the fridge to place a piece of plastic wrap directly onto the dressing to make sure no air is getting to your dressing.

French Dressing

Ingredients:

⅔ cup ketchup

¼ cup of a small onion

½ cup mayonnaise

⅓ cup red wine vinegar

1 teaspoon Worcestershire sauce

1 teaspoon paprika

½ teaspoon garlic powder

½ teaspoon Kosher salt

½ cup olive oil

White sugar to taste, I start with a tablespoon and add more if needed

Directions:

Add all ingredients except oil into the blender. Blend until smooth, gradually add your oil until you reach desired consistency, you can add a little bit of water to thin as well.

Raspberry Vinaigrette

Ingredients:

1 cup raspberries

1 tablespoon white sugar

⅔ cup balsamic vinegar

¼ cup olive oil

1 tablespoon honey

½ teaspoon salt

Directions:

    Sprinkle sugar on berries in a bowl and let sit for 10 minutes. Blend all ingredients in blender, add more oil and maybe a few sprinkles of water as needed for desired consistency

Italian Dressing

Ingredients:

1 cup extra virgin olive oil

⅓ cup red wine vinegar

½ teaspoon dried basil

1 teaspoon garlic powder (or use 1 clove fresh minced garlic)

1 teaspoon onion powder

¼ teaspoon dried thyme

½ teaspoon dried oregano

Optional: 1- teaspoons of honey or agave

Directions:

Mix ingredients and shake or blend well.

Asian Sweet and Spicy Dressing

Ingredients:

½ cup olive oil

Juice of one orange

2 tablespoons of honey

¼ cup rice wine vinegar

1 teaspoon of chili paste

1-2 teaspoons of sesame oil depending on your taste

Directions:

Mix ingredients and shake or blend well.

Mexican Dressing

Ingredients:

½ cup olive oil

¼ cup red wine vinegar

Juice of one lime

1 teaspoon chili powder

¼ teaspoon cumin

¼ teaspoon of garlic seasoning

Directions:

Mix ingredients and shake or blend well.

Mayonnaise

Mayonnaise is filled with preservatives and lots of added sugar. I love creating my own and it taste much better! I use farm fresh eggs that I get locally, but you can use store bought pasteurized eggs. The difference is how long you can keep the mayo in the fridge. If you use non-pasteurized eggs, it will last up to 6 months (although it has never lasted that long in my house). If you use pasteurized eggs. you must use your mayo within 1-2 weeks. Mayo can be tricky to make. I had many failed attempts at first. The key is making sure all your ingredients are at room temp before you start, including the eggs. Also, because you are using and consuming a raw egg, you must have acid in your mayo (vinegar and/or lemon juice). I highly recommend you watch some YouTube videos of all the many methods prior to your first attempt. You MUST be patient! If you try to rush any part of this process, you will have a runny mess. I first tried making mine in the food processor and then the blender (which gets too hot). Neither worked well for me. That is where the immersion blender comes in. I still had a few failures, but it now works most of the time. Patience is the key! Your mayo will be slightly warm, be sure to leave the lid off your mayo for a little bit in the fridge since. You do not moisture getting trapped in your container. I have used mason jars and condiment containers from the dollar store. However, my favorite way to store my mayo is to reuse store-bought mayo squeeze containers. Just clean them well and use a funnel to fill it with your own mayo.

Basic Mayo

Ingredients:

½ cup Extra light olive oil

1 teaspoon Dijon mustard or to taste (if you don't have fresh mustard you can you ground)

Sprinkle of salt/pepper

Small pinch of garlic powder

Juice of half a lemon

1 small splash of vinegar or to taste (I usually use apple cider, but white or red wine works well too)

If you want it to taste more like grocery store mayo than add a pinch of sugar. I never add sugar and it's delicious.

1 egg at room temperature. You can always place an egg in hot water for 5 mins to bring it to room temperature.

Directions:

Place all ingredients (make sure they are room temperature), into immersion blender container. Place your immersion blender flat on the bottom of the container over the egg. Pulse for one-second increments, waiting a few seconds in between pulses. If you do this step too fast, your mayo will break. You will see your emulsification start to build at the bottom. You should see little bubbles of it lifting off like a lava lamp. This takes a while- slowly pulsing while resting in-between pulses, this is where the patience comes in. Once the emulsification reaches just under the top of the oil, start to slowly lift your blender up and down to thoroughly mix the rest of the oil. It should look like thick mayo. However, if it did break and it is super runny, you can try to save it by adding another room temperature egg and start over with the pulsing.

Now let's take it to the next level with flavored mayo for wonderful sandwiches or sauces for pasta or macaroni salads.

Garlic mayo – So delicious!

Add some of your favorite garlic seasoning (or any seasoning for variety) or fresh roasted garlic to your mayo

Pesto Mayo- this one is a fan favorite!

Create a simple pesto using your immersion blender. Add some basil leaves, oil, salt, and a splash of lemon juice

(I rarely use pine nuts because they are so expensive). If you love Parmesan cheese, add a little bit of fresh grated cheese.

Blend it well until it's fully emulsified together. Add a tablespoon or two (until it has the flavor you like) to your pre-made mayo and mix well with spoon. You can store the left-over pesto in the fridge for a few days. You can use the leftover pesto on a chicken breast, top with tomato and cheese then bake- so yummy!

Inspiration

Inspiration

SALADS

I love salads! I eat them daily so that I do not get bored I change them up all the time. Salads are a great and versatile as you can switch up your ingredients and dressings to make them delicious and interesting. In this section all the basic ingredients will be listed, feel free to add or omit ingredients based on your liking. I hope these salads inspire you!

Asian Salad

This is one of my favorites! So many possibilities of things you could add in. Get creative!

Ingredients:

Romain Lettuce- You can use any type or mix of lettuce; however, I enjoy crunchy Romain for this salad

Chopped cilantro

Dried cranberries (or little mandarin orange slices are yummy too)

Sliced almonds

Chopped red pepper

Thinly sliced red onion

Edamame peas

Optional- chopped chicken

Directions:

Mix salad and use the sweet and spicy Asian dressing on page 46.

Strawberry Spinach Salad

This was a salad my dear friend Nikki had made for a family dinner and it is so delicious I just had to share it with you!

Ingredients:

2 cups rinsed, dried and coarsely chopped fresh spinach

1 half a red onion thinly sliced

1 cup sliced strawberries

Dressing:

⅓ cup olive oil

⅛ cup sugar

2 tablespoons vinegar

2 tablespoons sesame seeds

¼ teaspoon paprika

¼ teaspoon Worchester sauce (if vegan, omit)

Directions:

Mix dressing ingredients together and toss with fresh salad ingredients. Very yummy!

Mexican Salad

I really enjoy this salad, it provides a great change of pace from the norm and it taste wonderful too!

Ingredients:

Lettuce- Use your favorite lettuce or variety of lettuce

Chopped cilantro

Chopped red pepper

Chopped green pepper

Tomatoes

Beans- use your favorite canned rinsed beans

Thinly sliced red onion

Thin sliced tortilla strips

Optional- chopped cooked chicken, sliced cooked steak or hamburger taco meat for a taco salad

Directions:

Mix ingredients together and toss with Mexican salad dressing on page 47.

Cucumber Salad

This is a beautifully bright and delicious salad that can be altered to add your favorite ingredients. For added protein I will add some cooked Quinoa.

Ingredients:

3-4 cucumbers- diced to small bite size pieces

2-3 tomatoes – diced to same size as cucumber.

1 avocado- chopped in same size pieces

¼ cup chopped cilantro

¼ cup olive oil

⅛ cup red wine vinegar

1 teaspoon garlic seasoning

Dash of salt and pepper to taste

Optional- add some cooked, chilled quinoa for some added protein

Directions:

Mix all ingredients except avocado in a large bowl and toss with oil, vinegar, and seasonings. Chill in the fridge before serving. When ready to serve toss in the avocado. The avocado does not fare well in the fridge therefore I will make this salad and only add the avocado to the portion I am eating at that time.

Tomato salad

There are so many options for this kind of salad to omit or add fresh veggies, get creative! I love chopped celery in this too. This is a great side dish to so many meals.

Ingredients:

2-3 tomatoes- you can use any variety you like, chopped in bite size pieces. I often will use lots of cherry tomatoes and just slice them in half.

¼ of a red onion- sliced thin

1 avocado- chopped in bite size pieces

2 tablespoons Balsamic vinegar

4 tablespoons olive oil

Dash of salt and pepper to taste

Directions:

Mix all ingredients together and serve right away.

Coleslaw

This is a take-off from a traditional coleslaw. The apples give this a great little surprise with every bite. This is a great potluck side dish too. All the kids really love this coleslaw.

Ingredients:

1 bag of chopped slaw mix (or you can shred a head of cabbage)

1-2 green apples, peeled, cored, and chopped into bit size pieces

Dressing:

½ cup mayo

⅛ - ¼ cup apple cider vinegar (start with 1/8 as you can always add more to your liking)

A couple pinches of sugar to counteract the vinegar. You can always add more to your taste

Dash of salt and pepper to taste- I usually do not add salt but I add lots of pepper because I really like the vinegar, sour green apples, and pepper flavors together.

Directions:

Mix dressing, set aside. Combined apples and slaw in a bowl and pour dressing over, mix thoroughly. Refrigerate until ready to serve. This slaw is best if refrigerated for several hours to 1 day prior to serving.

Asian Coleslaw

I love this healthier (sugar free and dairy free) alternative to the traditional coleslaw. I could eat this as a main meal every day, it's very delicious!

Ingredients:

1 bag of chopped slaw mix (or you can shred a head of cabbage)
Sunflower seeds
Sesame seeds
Green Onions - chopped small
1-2 cucumbers- chopped small
⅛ cup chopped cilantro
¾ cup Asian Sweet and Spicy dressing on page 46

Directions:

Mix dressing, set aside. Combine all other fresh ingredients in a large bowl. Mix in dressing and sprinkle in the sunflower seeds and sesame seeds to taste. If you are looking to create this more as a main dish you could add some chopped cooked chicken as well.

Potato Salad

There are many varieties of potato salad, this is a basic recipe, feel free to get creative and add some of your favorite ingredients.

Ingredients:

3 pounds potatoes, peeled and chopped into bite size pieces

½ cup celery chopped or minced (your preference)

¼ cup minced onion (white, yellow, or purple- whichever you prefer)

1 cup of mayo

1 teaspoon Dijon mustard

Dash of salt and pepper to taste

Directions:

Boil potatoes just until slightly tender, be careful not to over-cook. Drain. I like to place the potatoes in a bowl and place in the fridge to cool. Chop your onion and celery set aside. Mix the mayo, mustard, salt and pepper. Mix everything together and chill for at least 2 hours before serving.

Optional add ins: chopped or sliced boiled eggs, minced carrots, fresh parsley, fresh dill, sweet relish, or cheese. Get creative!

Macaroni salad

There are many varieties of macaroni salad, this is a basic recipe, feel free to get creative and add some of your favorite ingredients.

Ingredients:

1 pound of your favorite pasta- I like using my fun shaped pasta but if it's not on hand I use Ditalini or Elbow

½ cup celery chopped or minced (your preference)

¼ cup minced onion (white, yellow, or purple- whichever you prefer)

1 cup of mayo

1 teaspoon Dijon mustard

Dash of salt and pepper to taste

Directions:

Boil pasta just until slightly tender, be careful not to over-cook. Drain. I like to place the pasta in a bowl and place in the fridge to cool overnight if possible. Chop your onion and celery set aside. Mix the mayo, mustard, salt and pepper. Mix everything together and chill for at least 2 hours before serving.

Optional add ins: chopped or sliced boiled eggs, minced carrots, fresh parsley, fresh dill, sweet relish, chopped red pepper, olives, or cheese. Get creative!

Italian Pasta Salad

There are many varieties of Italian pasta salad, this is a basic recipe, feel free to get creative and add some of your favorite ingredients.

Ingredients:

1 pound of your favorite pasta- I like using my fun shaped pasta but if it's not on hand I use Bow Tie or Rotini

1 cup broccoli florets

1 cup of diced tomatoes or halved cherry tomatoes

1 ½ cup diced cucumber

¼ cup red onion

1 can sliced black olives

1 package frozen artichoke hearts- thawed and chopped fine

1 ½ cup Italian Dressing on page 45

Directions:

Boil pasta just until slightly tender, be careful not to over-cook. Drain. I like to place the pasta in a bowl and place in the fridge to cool overnight if possible. Chop your veggies and set aside. Mix everything together and chill for at least 2 hours before serving.

Optional add ins: fresh parsley, fresh basil, chopped red pepper, green olives, bell pepper, various Italian meats, and

Mozzarella cut into small cubes and or shredded Parmesan cheese. Get creative!

Tabouli

This is a little time consuming but so worth it! I do not recommend you chop the veggies in the food processor as it will turn them to mush. The smaller and finer you chop the ingredients the better. It's best to make a day ahead as all the flavors mingle and it tastes so much better.

Ingredients:

1 head romaine lettuce

1 English cucumber chopped into fine pieces

1 cucumber, peeled and sliced

4 green onions

12 fresh mint leaves

2 bunches of parsley

4 Roma tomatoes

1 head of romaine lettuce

3 tablespoons of lemon juice

3 tablespoons of extra virgin olive oil

½ cup Bulgur wheat, fine

Directions:

Proper care and cleaning of the parsley for this dish is the time-consuming part. You should sit down with a bowl and relax while you pull leaf by leaf of the parsley off and discard the stems. Put the leaves in a salad spinner (or use a colander and bowl) fill the spinner with water and let the leaves soak for a bit giving them a stir every now and then. This is an important step as it removes all the dirt that hides underneath the leaves. Once you pull the parsley up out of the water you will see how dirty the water is. I usually do this rinse twice. Once rinsed drain the water and spin the parsley dry or spread on a towel to dry and then chop fine.

Place the Bulgar Wheat in a cup with some water for about 10 minutes then squeeze the water out. Place all the ingredients (expect lettuce and sliced cucumber) in a bowl and mix thoroughly.

Serve with romaine lettuce boats and or cucumber slices. Tabouli is great with hummus too!

Cowboy Caviar

This is a dish that is eaten as a dip and is a crowd pleaser for sure! I will bring this to potlucks and it gets gobbled up every time.

Ingredients:

1-15 ounce can black beans

1-15 ounce can black-eyed peas

1 cup chopped cilantro

1 cup thawed frozen corn (or fresh cooked and chilled)

½ cup chopped green pepper

½ cup chopped red pepper

1 small chopped red onion

1-pound Roma tomatoes diced

2 diced avocados

½ cup olive oil

¼ cup white wine vinegar

1 teaspoon chili powder

1 teaspoon cumin

½ teaspoon garlic powder

¼ cup sugar (optional)- I usually just use a pinch of sugar

Salt and pepper to taste

Directions:

In a large bowl, whisk together olive oil, sugar, white

wine vinegar, chili powder, cumin, and garlic. Drain and rinse black beans and peas. Add tomatoes, beans, peas, corn, onion, and peppers to combine. Stir in cilantro and salt and pepper to taste. Cover and chill for at least 1 hour or overnight.

Right before serving add the chopped avocado. Serve with tortilla chips.

Cranberry Chicken Salad

This is great served as lunch. You can use leftover cooked chicken breast, canned chicken, or rotisserie chicken. You can serve this with lettuce cups, chopped lettuce as a salad, crackers, croissants, or your favorite kind of bread.

Ingredients:

2 cups chopped chicken

½ cup mayo

¼ cup dried cranberries

1-2 stalks of celery finely sliced

Salt and Pepper to taste

Optional- sliced almonds

Directions:

Mix everything together and refrigerate before serving. If you are adding the almonds I recommend you add them right before serving as they will get soft.

Inspiration

DIPS & SALSA

You can make many of these recipes for your guests. However, sometimes I just make them for myself as a lunchtime meal and snack throughout the week. I love to snack; these recipes are just perfect for that!

Hummus

Hummus is so easy to make and there are so many things you can add in for many delicious options.

Ingredients:

2 cans garbanzo beans drained and rinsed

2 cloves of peeled garlic

¼ cup olive oil

2 tablespoons of lemon juice

2 tablespoons of Tahini

⅛- ¼ cup of water

Salt to taste

Directions:

Place all ingredients in the blender, you may need to add more oil and/or water to get the desired consistency. It will get a little thicker once chilled. Chill in the fridge before serving. I serve hummus with bell peppers (green and red), baby carrots, sliced cucumbers, hummus is great with Tabouli too!

Optional add ins- use roasted garlic instead of fresh, roasted red pepper, roasted jalapenos, cilantro, beets, spinach and feta cheese, artichokes hearts with fresh herbs, and sun-dried tomato and basil. You can get so creative with a basic hummus recipe.

Spinach Dip

This recipe is loaded with sodium. I usually only make it around the holiday because it is an all-time favorite at my house. My family begs me to make it every chance they can get. My recipe has bacon in it and it's one of the few times I eat bacon anymore. It takes this spinach dip to a whole new level. If bacon is not in your diet, you can always omit it. I usually make the entire batch and save a little without the bacon for those that do not eat bacon. This is a double batch so if you are making it for a small group than you will want to half this recipe. In my house if there is any leftover it doesn't last long.

Ingredients:

2 packages of Knorr Spring Vegetable Soup Mix, sometimes I am not able to find SPRING vegetable mix, I will just get the regular vegetable soup mix

2 cans water chestnuts- rinsed, drained and chopped finely

2 boxes of frozen spinach, thawed and drained

2 cups of mayonnaise

20 ounces. of sour cream

1 package of bacon

Directions:

Cook your bacon, cool and chop. I like to cook it crunchy because it will be in the sauce to soften it up. Rinse, drain and chop your chestnuts. With the frozen spinach, I usually place it in the fridge in a bowl the day before, so it will thaw. When you are ready to use it, it is important to squeeze all the moisture out of it before adding it to your dip or else you will have a soupy mess.

In a large mixing bowl combine the mayo, sour cream, and soup mix and stir well. Add your chestnuts and spinach, stir well. This is where I would reserve some of the dip in another bowl for those that do not wish to have bacon. Add your bacon and stir. Chill for a few hours or overnight before serving.

You can create a fancy bread bowl to place it in for presentation. I do not do this anymore as no one at my house ever eats it anyway and I hate wasting food! I usually serve it with a variety of chopped vegetable and crackers. My family loves crunchy Trisquits with their dip.

Ranch Dip

If you buy pre-packaged ranch seasoning it is loaded with preservatives and chemical binders. It is easy to make your own seasoning mix and add it to sour cream, mayo or sprinkle on chicken for dinner. I also have used this seasoning to make a healthier version of ranch dressing using almond milk and avocados, add this mix to it and it taste just like ranch and it's thick and creamy too. I will make a big batch of this seasoning and keep in my pantry so it is ready when I need it.

Seasoning Ingredients:

½ tablespoon black pepper

1 teaspoon garlic powder

1 tablespoon parsley flakes

1 teaspoon dry minced onions

1 teaspoon onion powder

1 tablespoon

Directions:

To make Ranch Dip add a teaspoon (or more to taste) to 1 cup of sour cream. Chill before serving.

Pico Salsa

Who doesn't love salsa? This is a basic recipe you can always add more or less jalapenos depending on how hot you like it. You can use these same ingredients to create a chunky or thinner salsa.

Ingredients:

1- 2 pounds chopped tomatoes

1-2 chopped jalapenos (depends on your taste)

¼ cup chopped cilantro

1-2 cloves garlic

½ onion chopped finely

Salt and pepper to taste

Directions:

This is where a food processor or chopper comes in. You can prepare all ingredients except tomatoes in the food processor. Combine them all in a large bowl, chill before serving. If you want chunky Pico salsa then you do not want to put tomatoes in the food processor or blender. However, if you like your salsa smooth then go ahead and all the ingredients into your processor or blender. This salsa is great to use with chips, to add to your Mexican feast, or to top grilled chicken or fish with!

Guacamole

Oh, how I love avocados! Guacamole is super easy to make and is delicious.

Ingredients:

4-6 avocados, peeled, pitted and diced

½ teaspoon dried or chopped fresh oregano

½ cup Pico Salsa on page 78

¼ teaspoon oregano

Salt to taste

Directions:

Place diced avocado in a large bowl. Using a fork and a knife chop/mush until desired consistency. I like my guacamole a little chunky. If you like yours smoother, place in the food processor. Mix in your Pico salsa to taste. Add some salt and oregano to taste. Avocado will turn brown quickly so serve right away. If you are not serving it right away you can place your guacamole in a bowl and press a piece of plastic wrap directly onto the guacamole so there is not air that can reach it, place a lid on the bowl and refrigerate.

Inspiration

APPETIZERS

Appetizers are a great snack for any party. Although, you do not need an excuse to create these fabulous creations. These are great for a snack, a party, lunch, or potluck.

Bruschetta

I love bruschetta! So fresh and so light, it makes a great appetizer, served with bread or top your cooked chicken or fish with it and you won't be disappointed.

Ingredients:

1-2 pounds tomatoes

¼ cup fresh chopped basil, more if you desire

¼ of a small onion chopped fine (purple or white)

1 clove garlic finely minced

A drizzle of olive oil

1 teaspoon vinegar (red wine or balsamic- whichever you prefer. I like to use red wine and drizzle with a balsamic glaze right before serving).

Salt and pepper to taste

Directions:

Mix all ingredients in a large bowl. Salt and pepper to taste. Serve on toasted bread, drizzle with balsamic glaze if desired. For Balsamic glaze- place ¼ cup balsamic vinegar in a sauce pan, bring to a boil and let it reduce. Be sure to keep an eye on it as it can burn easily, stir often. It's ready when it starts to coat your spoon. Remove from heat and let it cool a bit. It will get thicker as it cools. Drizzle away!

Shrimp Ceviche

Most recipes call for raw shrimp as the acids in the juices will cook the shrimp. I always boil my shrimp, cook it and dice it. Either way works well, just don't boil for too long as your shrimp will be tough. It only needs a couple of minutes in the boiling water then transfer to an ice bath right away.

Ingredients:

1 cup orange juice

¼ cup lime

¼ cup lemon

1 pound cooked diced shrimp

½ a bunch Cilantro

1-2 diced cucumbers

1-2 large tomatoes

½ diced purple onion

3 serrano chilies finely minced

Salt/Pepper

Olive Oil

1 Avocado- diced

Directions:

Add all ingredients (except avocado) in a large bowl, mix thoroughly. This is best when it had time for the flavors to mingle so I like to make it the day ahead. Just be sure to add the avocado right before serving. Serve with tortilla chips.

Stuffed Mushrooms

I have two ways I commonly prepare my mushrooms, one with sausage and one meatless version. These are a thanksgiving staple at our house. They are easy to prep the day before to save time when you have guest, just cook and serve!

Sausage Stuffed Mushrooms

Ingredients:

2 dozen whole fresh mushrooms, you can use white button or baby bellas

¼ cup minced onion

1 tablespoon minced garlic

½ pound ground sausage

¼ cup bread crumbs

¼ cup butter

1- 8 ounce package of softened cream cheese

¾ cup Mozzarella cheese

¼ cup melted butter

Pepper to taste

Directions:

Preheat oven to 325 degrees. Clean the mushrooms well, removing stems and save for later. Dry mushrooms with a paper towel and place in a baking dish ready to stuff. Remove the tough ends of the stems and place into food processor to chop fine. Cook sausage, breaking into small crumbles. Remove to a paper towel to absorb most of the grease, reserving 2 tablespoons of the grease in the pan. Add onion and stem pieces to the grease, cook until all moisture is gone, add garlic and cook for 1 minute. Remove from heat and let cool.

In a large mixing bowl, stir in cream cheese, sausage, bread crumbs, ¼ cup cheese, black pepper, and mushroom stems. Stuff the mixture into the mushroom caps and top with additional cheese. Drizzle each mushroom with butter and bake for 30 minutes until golden brown.

Veggie Stuffed Mushrooms

Ingredients:

2 dozen whole fresh mushrooms, you can use white button or baby bellas

¼ cup minced onion

¼ cup minced celery

1 tablespoon minced garlic

¼ cup bread crumbs

¼ cup butter

¾ cup Mozzarella cheese

¼ cup melted butter

Pepper to taste

Directions:

Preheat oven to 325 degrees. Clean the mushrooms well, removing stems and save for later. Dry mushrooms with a paper towel and place in a baking dish ready to stuff. Remove the tough ends of the stems and place into food processor to chop fine. Melt butter in a pan, add onion, celery, and stem pieces, cook until all transparent add garlic and cook for 1 minute. Add bread crumbs and mix until mixture is somewhat crumbly. You may have to add a bit more bread crumbs to get the texture you like.

Remove from heat and let cool. Stir in ¼ cup Mozzarella cheese. Stuff the mixture into the mushroom caps and top with additional cheese. Drizzle each mushroom with butter and bake for 30 minutes until golden brown.

Add in ideas: chopped spinach, fresh herbs like oregano, and fresh Parmesan cheese if you prefer.

Blackened Shrimp Avocado Cucumber Bites

These are a light slightly spicy appetizer that is easy to prepare and easy to impress your guests with. They are super delicious, I just love the little bit of heat combined with the coolness of the avocado and cucumber.

Ingredients:

1 tablespoon oil

1 tablespoon creole seasoning

1-pound shrimp, peeled and de-veined

1 cucumber sliced

1 avocado mashed

1 green onion chopped fine

2 tablespoons cilantro or parsley chopped fine

1 tablespoon lemon juice

Salt and Cayenne to taste

Directions:

Toss the shrimp in the oil and seasoning in a pre-heated (medium-high heat) skillet until slightly blackened, about 2-3 minutes per side. Create avocado sauce by mixing avocado, green onion and cilantro. Assemble the bites with cucumber slices, topped with avocado sauce, then shrimp.

Vegetable Tortilla Roll Ups

Here is light snack that everyone seems to devour. These are great for any luncheon or potluck. You can change these up in so many ways by adding your favorite vegetables, make it to your liking!

Ingredients:

1 cup baby spinach

2 tablespoons orange bell pepper chopped fine

½ English cucumber halved and sliced thin

2 green onions thinly sliced

2 tablespoons fresh chopped parsley

2 radishes thinly sliced

4 flour tortillas (you could use any variety, like spinach- yum!)

1- 8-ounce package of softened cream cheese

Pepper to taste

Directions:

In a large mixing bowl, combine cream cheese, bell pepper, parsley, and green onions. Spread ¼ of the mixture each tortilla. In rows, add spinach, cucumber, and radish. Roll into a log shape, cover with plastic wrap and refrigerate at least an hour or overnight. Unwrap and slice.

With this recipe you leave some veggies in large pieces then roll it up, you could chop all your veggies (any of your choice) fine and mix it all together with the cream cheese, there are no rules!

Kim Richardson

Inspiration

Inspiration

QUINOA

Quinoa is so versatile, it really has become my new favorite kitchen staple. You can cook it with chicken broth or vegetable broth instead of water to infuse it with flavor. I like to use my rice cooker and cook up a big batch to heat up and add to my salads during the week for added protein. You can use it as a side dish or make it the make show for your next meal. It is gluten free, loaded with protein and has a low Glycemic Index so it's much better for you than any pasta or rice.

Quinoa with potatoes

This is one of Paula Obeid's recipes and everyone always asks her to make it for them; including me, it's so simple and delicious!

Ingredients:

2 cups cooked quinoa

3-4 potatoes, peeled and chopped in bite size pieces

1 red pepper, diced

½ small onion, diced

Olive oil

Salt and pepper to taste

Directions:

Fry your potatoes in a little bit of olive oil until tender (or if you have an air fryer use that!). Remove potatoes and set aside. Add another small drizzle of oil to the pan and stir fry the onions, peppers. Sprinkle with a little salt and pepper. Once cooked to desired consistency add the potatoes and Quinoa into the pan. Mix thoroughly and season with salt and pepper. Serve warm.

You can add all kinds of veggies to this dish, I love mushrooms, yellow squash and zucchini too. I like to cook large batches of this and place in freezer bags and freeze for a quick meal anytime.

Quinoa Vegan Tacos

Paula's daughter, Sarah Obeid made this for me when I went to visit, and it was so delicious! Everyone always loves these! They make a great substitute for hamburger taco meat. Serve with freshly cooked tortillas, crunchy taco shells or tostadas, or just eat as is.

Ingredients:

1 cup cooked quinoa

½ cup cauliflower rice (raw cauliflower placed into the food processor until it is fine and resembles rice)

½ cup of your favorite salsa, I like to use my Pico salsa recipe

2- tablespoons fresh cilantro

2 teaspoons ground cumin

2 teaspoon ground chili powder

½ teaspoon garlic powder

2 tablespoon nutritional yeast (optional- it just gives it a cheesy flavor)

Salt and pepper to taste

Directions:

Pre-heat oven 375 degrees. Mix all ingredients except nutritional yeast in a bowl. Spread mixture onto a parchment lined backing sheet, the thinner you spread it the better it will cook. Sprinkle the top with the nutritional yeast. Bake for about 40 mins, check it… sometimes you must cook it longer. Give it a stir with a spatula, it should be drying out, be a crumbly texture and look like hamburger taco meat when it's done.

Serve with all the preferred taco toppings like lettuce, tomato, onions, guacamole, sour cream, or cheese.

Thai Quinoa

This is another great dish that everyone gobbles right up! When I do this for catering I will keep all the toppings separate and let everyone build their own. Add or omit any of your favorite veggies.

Ingredients:

¾ cup cooked quinoa

1-2 cups shredded red cabbage

1 red bell pepper

½ red onion

1 cup shredded carrots

¼ cup green onions

½ cup chopped cashews

1 cup edamame beans

Fresh lime

Dressing:

¼ cup peanut butter

2 teaspoons of ginger

3 tablespoons soy sauce

1 tablespoon honey

1 tablespoon red wine vinegar

1 teaspoon sesame oil

1 teaspoon olive oil

Water to thin

Directions:

Mix dressing ingredients and set aside. In a large bowl mix quinoa and veggies then dressing and serve.

Caprese Quinoa Skillet

This is a great hearty vegetarian main dish. You can use vegan cheese for a dairy free option as well.

Ingredients:

1 ½ cooked quinoa

½ cup extra virgin olive oil

½ cup fresh basil

2 tablespoons lemon juice

3 garlic gloves

½ teaspoon ground black pepper

2 large tomatoes sliced ¼' thick

1 ball Mozzarella sliced (or use vegan Mozzarella)

½ cup balsamic vinegar

Directions:

Mix olive oil, basil, lemon juice, garlic, salt, and pepper in a bowl and pour over cooked quinoa. In an oven safe skillet like cast iron, place the quinoa on the bottom, layer the tomato slices then top with cheese slices. Drizzle with oil and salt and pepper. Place under broiler until cheese is melted about 5 minutes. Remove and drizzle with balsamic glaze and garnish with fresh chopped basil.

For Balsamic glaze- place ¼ cup balsamic vinegar in a sauce pan, bring to a boil and let it reduce. Be sure to keep an eye on it as it can burn easily, stir often. It's ready when it starts to coat your spoon. Remove from heat and let it cool a bit. It will get thicker as it cools. Drizzle away!

Mexican Quinoa Bowls

This is such a light refreshing, healthy meal and makes a great lunch for your meal prepping too!

Ingredients:

3 chicken breasts

½ package of grape tomatoes, quartered

2 cups cooked quinoa

2 tablespoon chopped cilantro

½ lime

1 cup of corn

1 avocado cored and chopped

1 can Rotel tomatoes (or use Pico recipe)

1 tablespoon chili powder

1 tablespoon cumin

½ teaspoon garlic seasoning

1 tablespoon olive oil

½ tablespoon of red wine vinegar

Directions:

Preheat oven to 400 degrees. Place chicken in a baking dish, sprinkle with chili powder, cumin, and garlic seasoning. Bake for 25 mins or until no longer pink and slice thin or chop in bite size pieces. While chicken is cooking, place the Rotel in blender to a fine puree and pour in a sauce pan. Stir in about ½ tablespoon of cumin and chili powder and bring to a simmer until it thickens just a bit. Heat the corn at the same time. In a large mixing bowl, mix the quinoa, corn, sauce. Pour in the lime juice and give it a stir. Add in cilantro, tomatoes, and chicken. Sprinkle with the olive oil and vinegar and mix thoroughly.

Top each serving with the avocado right before serving. If desired sprinkle with some chopped cilantro.

Kim Richardson

Inspiration

BREAKFAST

I never used to eat breakfast, however I have since changed that bad habit. I usually have something light; oatmeal and an apple, a smoothie, or a prepared frozen egg bake. I love preparing heart shaped breakfast items. You can use cookie cutters or fun cooking molds for biscuits, pancakes, or frying an egg. Sometimes I'll fry an egg just for myself in a heart shape … just because that's high vibe eating. There are all kinds of cooking and baking molds available in all kinds of fun shapes.

Amaretto French Toast Bake

This is a bread pudding type recipe that has been altered to use it as a breakfast casserole. This works great when you have a large group for breakfast and everyone always loves it.

Ingredients:

Day old loaf white bread, cubed

½ quart half-and-half

½ cup sugar

6 eggs

1 tablespoon almond or vanilla extract

½ cup almonds, sliced

Sauce:

½ cup butter

1 cup powdered sugar

2-3 tablespoons cup amaretto liqueur

Directions:

Mix half and half, sugar, eggs, and almond extract in large mixing bowl and whisk together. Stir in bread cubes, cover with foil and let set in fridge overnight. Preheat oven to 350 degrees. Give it a good mix and then pour into a buttered 9 x 13-inch pan. Bake for 35-40 mins or until set. I like to sprinkle the almonds over the top about 15 minutes before it is done. Use a knife to poke the center to see if it comes out clean- that's when it's done.

When your French toast bake is almost finished baking, place butter in a saucepan and melt slowly. Add powdered sugar. Cook until smooth and incorporated. Add amaretto liqueur.

Cut into squares and serve warm with warmed sauce. The sauce is sweet, so I like to leave it on the side for people to add the amount they like. You can always use maple syrup as well.

Egg Bakes

These are easy a great way to serve a large group of people. You can add whatever ingredients you like to customize your egg bake to your liking. I use muffin pans that have been sprayed with nonstick cooking spray. These are also great to make ahead and freeze so you will have a quick breakfast throughout the week.

Here is the basic egg bake- Use scramble eggs. Usually about 6 eggs will make 6 egg bakes.

Directions:

Pre-heat oven to 350 degrees. Add whichever toppings you would like to the muffin pan, pour eggs over toppings and bake for 20-25 minutes. Some ingredients you may want to sauté first; ham, various veggies, etc.

Green Chili- use a can of diced green chilies, mix with your scrambled eggs then bake. You can add some turkey sausage crumbles and shredded cheese if desired or mix all ingredients together. Bake in a larger pan, cook time will be around 30-40 minutes. I top with cheese during the last 10 minutes of cooking when making in a large pan.

For my veggie egg bakes, I will chop some mushrooms and onions and sauté, add chopped fresh spinach right at the end just to heat/wilt a little bit. I will add the mixture to the bottom of muffin pan and top with scrambled eggs and shredded cheese if desired. It's easy and fun to create fun shapes using cookie cutters; bake your scrambled egg bakes with whichever toppings desired in a large lasagna size pan and bake. Once they are done cooking use your cookie cutters. So fun to have heart shaped egg bakes!

Smoothies

I love smoothies! I love getting creative, I will start throwing stuff right in my blender. Most of the time my creations turn out great. However, there are sometimes when it's not so great. How do you know if you don't try! I encourage you to get creative with these basic smoothie recipes. I will rinse, dry, cut up and freeze all my fruit and veggies in individual bags so I can just easily throw a smoothie together. You could go one step further and add all your smoothie ingredients in one bag, so it is even easier. I do not peel them or cut of the stems as they have much of the nutrients in them stems and leaves.

If you have a good blender it will blend up everything to a super smooth texture. I have even put an entire avocado seed in my smoothies; they are packed with good nutrients! Do not try to put an avocado seed in an average blender or it will break, you must have a powerful one like a Blend Tec or Vitamix.

Optional add ins for additional benefits: Chia Seeds, Flax Seed, Spirulina Powder, and Wheat Germ.

Liquids: milk, almond milk, coconut milk, yogurt, any fruit juice; apple, orange, pineapple, pomegranate, or just use some water and/or a little ice to give it a thicker consistency.

To create any smoothie, add your favorite fruit and veggies and a little bit of liquid and blend well.

Here are some of my favorite combinations, and if you want to sneak in a bit more nutrients, add a little kale or spinach to any smoothie.

Fruit Smoothies:

- Strawberry and banana with 1 cup of fruit juice or milk of choice
- Strawberry, banana with orange juice and a small piece of ginger root.
- Carrot juice, pineapple, and mango
- Mango, strawberry, banana, and orange juice

Green smoothies:

You may think green smoothies are not delicious, however, you can add a few things to make them taste great; honey, agave, and/or pineapple. Green apple, and ginger root are some of my favorite things to add.

- Banana, spinach, blueberries, water
- Kale or spinach, pineapple, ginger root, and milk of choice
- Kale or spinach, Pineapple, avocado (minus the skin), ice cubes, and water.

BREADS

Breads are a special treat! Keep your pantry stocked with flour, sugar, vanilla, and apple sauce and you will always have just about everything you need to create these wonderful treats. I will buy fruits/veggies when they are in season and freeze them so I can enjoy them year-round. You may notice I said; apple sauce ... yes, apple sauce makes a great substitute for vegetable oil. It not only works great for baking it will make your creations super moist.

Pumpkin Bread

I love everything pumpkin! I do not always wait for fall to get my pumpkin fix and this bread is a delicious, not to sweet way to fulfill my pumpkin desires.

Ingredients:

½ cup softened butter

1 cup brown sugar

1 can pumpkin puree

2 eggs

1 ½ teaspoon cinnamon

½ teaspoon pumpkin pie spice

1 teaspoon baking powder

1 teaspoon baking soda

½ teaspoon salt

1 ½ cups all-purpose flour

Directions:

Preheat oven to 350 degrees. Grease a 9" loaf pan with cooking spray and set aside. In a large bowl combine all the ingredients and beat at medium speed until well mixed. Pour the mixture into the loaf pan and bake for 4-50 minutes or until a toothpick inserted near the center comes out clean. Be careful not to overcook.

Zucchini Bread

When zucchini is in season I love making this bread. Even when it's not in season I will shred the zucchini or yellow squash and freeze it for later. If you freeze it, you will lose some volume as it thaws so I usually freeze an extra ½ cup than what the recipe calls for in pre-measured baggies. I will sometimes make muffins instead of a whole bread, the cook time will be much less, be sure to check muffins in 20-30 minutes.

Ingredients:

2 ¼ cup sugar

1 cup apple sauce

3 eggs

3 teaspoon vanilla extract

2 cups grated zucchini

3 cups all-purpose flour

3 teaspoons cinnamon

1 teaspoon salt

1 teaspoon baking soda

1 teaspoon baking powder

Directions:

    Preheat oven to 325 degrees. Grease two loaf pans and set aside. In a large bowl combine; sugar, apple sauce, eggs and vanilla. In a separate bowl mix your dry ingredients; flour, cinnamon, salt, baking soda and baking powder. Slowly mix the dry ingredients into the wet until combined, do not over mix. Stir in zucchini. Pour into loaf pans and bake for 45-55 minutes or until a toothpick inserted near the center comes out clean.

Lemon Blueberry Zucchini Bread

I decided to give this a try one day and I am not sure if I will ever make plain zucchini bread again. It's so delicious everyone gobbles it up quick and now I am sure to make a double batch every time.

Ingredients:

3 eggs

1 cup apple sauce

1 tablespoon vanilla extract

2 ¼ cups white sugar

2 cups shredded zucchini or yellow squash (or a mixture of both)

3 cups all-purpose flour

1 teaspoon salt

1 teaspoon baking powder

¼ teaspoon baking soda

1 pint fresh or frozen blueberries (frozen works better for baking)

Lemon Glaze:

1 cup powdered sugar

1 tablespoon fresh lemon juice

1 tablespoon heavy whipping cream

Directions:

Preheat oven to 350 degrees. Lightly grease 2 large loaf pans. In a large bowl, beat together; eggs, apple sauce, vanilla, and sugar. Fold in the zucchini. In separate smaller bowl mix the dry ingredients; flour, salt, baking powder, and baking soda. Beat the dry ingredients into the wet until mixed well. Gently fold in the blueberries. Pour into loaf pans and bake for 40-50 minutes or until a toothpick inserted near the center comes out clean. Be careful not to overcook or your bread will be very dry.

While bread is cooling prepare the glaze; Whisk all the ingredients for the glaze together and once the bread is well cooled (at least 20 minutes), drizzle the glaze over the top of the bread.

Blueberry muffins

Blueberry muffins are always a hit with any crowd. I love blueberries and will often stock up when they are in season and on sale. They freeze wonderfully to use in my smoothies or muffin recipes.

Ingredients:

1 ½ cups all purples flour

¾ cup granulated sugar

½ teaspoon baking powder

⅓ cup apple sauce

⅓- ½ cup of milk

1 ½ teaspoons vanilla extract

1 cup of fresh or frozen blueberries (frozen really holds up better when baking)

Directions:

Preheat oven to 400 degrees. Grease muffin tins and set aside. In a large bowl, combined flour, sugar, baking soda, and salt. In a separate bowl mix sugar, apple sauce, egg, vanilla, and milk. Slowly add flour to wet mixture, do not over mix. Mixture will be thick. Gently fold in blueberries. Add mixture to muffin tins and bake for about 15-20 minutes. Check the doneness by inserting a knife.

Banana Bread

I love banana bread especially when it's not too sweet. This recipe creates a super moist wonderful bread that is so delicious!

Ingredients:

2 cups sugar

1 cup softened butter

5 eggs

2 cups all-purpose flour

6 tablespoons buttermilk

2 teaspoons baking soda

1 ½ cups very ripe, very brown and soft bananas

Optional: 1 cup chopped nuts

Directions:

Preheat oven to 350 degrees. Grease 2 loaf pans and set aside. In a large bowl mix all the wet ingredients first; butter, eggs, buttermilk, and bananas. Add sugar and mix well. Mix in flour and baking soda. Optional, stir in nuts. Let the mixture sit cover for 1 hour. Pour into loaf pans and bake 50-60 minutes or until a toothpick inserted neat the center of the loaf comes of clean. The top may become very brown, do not worry it will still be so delicious. Let cool before serving.

Orange Cranberry Muffins

The kids love these muffins! You can make muffins or create a bread to slice; you will just need to adjust the cook time.

Ingredients:

4 cups all-purpose flour

2 teaspoons baking soda

1 ½ teaspoon salt

2 cups sugar (plus ¼ cup for cranberries)

4 cups fresh or frozen thawed cranberries cut in half

2 tablespoons orange jest

2 eggs

1 cup orange juice

1 cup water

⅔ cup apple sauce

Optional: 2 cups chopped nuts

Directions:

Preheat oven to 350 degrees. Grease 2 loaf pans or muffin tins. Place halved cranberries in a bowl and mix with ¼ cup of sugar, set aside. Mix together flour, baking soda, and salt, set aside. In a separate bowl, mix together sugar, orange rind, and apple sauce add in eggs and mix. Slowly add flour mixture, orange juice and water to sugar mixture. Once mixed together add cranberries and nuts. If making a loaf, bake for 35 minutes and start checking for doneness, mostly likely it will need about 45 minutes. If making muffins, start checking for doneness around 25 minutes. To check if they are ready insert a knife or toothpick into the center and if it comes out clean they are ready.

Kim Richardson

Inspiration

SOUP

Oh, How I love soup! Most soups are quick and easy to make, and I love making huge batches, so I can eat the leftovers throughout the week. You will notice I usually chop most of my vegetables pretty small/minced, however if you like them chunkier then you can cut them whichever way you would like. I just find that even my picky eaters usually do not mind the ingredients that may otherwise not like if they are chopped small. You can choose to use the soup as a side for your dinner or make it shine as the main dish. If serving as the main dish, serve with salad and garlic bread or just the bread is great too!

Minestrone Soup

This is a healthy, vegan recipe that can be adapted to your liking. Need gluten free option? Use gluten free pasta or omit the pasta all together.

Ingredients:

3 cups reduced-sodium vegetable or chicken broth

1 (28-ounce) can diced tomatoes

1 (15-ounce) can white (cannellini or navy) beans, drained

2 carrots, peeled and chopped

1 celery stalk, chopped

1 cup onion, chopped

1 teaspoon dried thyme

½ teaspoon dried sage

2 bay leaves

Salt and ground black pepper

2 cups cooked Ditalini pasta- I like to use fun shaped pasta like hearts or peace signs.

1 medium zucchini, chopped

2 cups coarsely chopped fresh spinach

4 tablespoons grated Parmesan or Romano cheese (if vegan, omit the cheese or use vegan cheese)

Basil sprigs, garnish, optional

Directions:

In a slow cooker, combine broth, tomatoes, beans, carrots, celery, onion, thyme, sage, bay leaves, and 1/2 teaspoon each salt and black pepper. Cover and cook on LOW for 6 to 8 hours or on HIGH for 3 to 4 hours.

Thirty minutes before the soup is done cooking add zucchini and spinach and pasta. Cover and cook 30 more minutes. Remove bay leaves and season, to taste, with salt and black pepper. Ladle soup into bowls and sprinkle Parmesan cheese over top. Garnish with basil, if desired.

Sausage Potato Soup

This is my version of Olive Garden's Zuppa Toscano Soup. It has a slight bit of heat to it with the cayenne pepper, so you can choose to spice it up depending on your taste. I like to use regular sausage because it is plenty hot for me with just the seasoning.

Ingredients:

1-pound breakfast sausage (you can use spicy or Italian sausage if you prefer)

4-6 russet potatoes, thinly sliced (I like to leave the peel on)

1 onion, chopped

2 tablespoons garlic, minced

32 ounces chicken broth

½ bunch kale (or Swiss Chard), de-stemmed and cut/torn into bite-sized pieces

1 cup heavy whipping cream

2 tablespoons flour

Salt and pepper to taste

Cayenne pepper to taste

¼ teaspoon red pepper flakes

Directions:

Brown sausage in a sauté pan. Place sausage, chicken broth, garlic, potatoes and onion in slow cooker. Add just enough water to cover the vegetables and meat. Cook on high 3-4 hours (low 5-6 hours) until potatoes are soft.
30 minutes before serving:

Mix flour into cream removing lumps. Add cream and kale to the crock pot, stir. Cook on high 30 minutes or until broth thickens slightly. Add salt, pepper, and cayenne to taste.

Optional: Top with bacon immediately before serving.

Creamy Chicken and Wild Rice

I love this hearty soup for a cold winter night! It's so easily done in the crock pot and ready in 4 hours. It can be low-fat and dairy free (if you make it without the cream or use almond milk) and gluten free. As with any soup you can omit the chicken and add whichever veggies you would like.

Ingredients:

1 pound of chicken breast

½ onion, minced

2 carrots, shredded and minced

3 celery stalks, minced

3 garlic gloves, minced

Salt and pepper to taste

½ teaspoon of dried thyme

¼ teaspoon dried sage

1 or 2 bay leaves

6 cups chicken broth

¾ cup uncooked wild rice

1 cup of heavy cream

Directions:

Rinse the rice then place all ingredients except the cream in the crock pot. Cook on high for 4 hours. Shred the chicken right in the crock pot and add the cream. Serve with garlic bread.

Optional add ins: Any veggies, however for softer veggies like mushrooms and squash put them in during the last two hours of cooking so they do not turn to mush. If you love bacon fry it and chop it and add it to the soup.

Creamy Chicken and Tortellini Soup

This has become one of my favorites and it's quick to make too! I will often buy a rotisserie chicken to speed up the process and it's delicious too. If you are not loving the meat, simply omit it and add whichever veggies you love.

Ingredients:

1 tablespoon of olive oil

1 large onion, chopped fine

1 red bell pepper, seeded and chopped fine

2 carrots, peeled and chopped fine

3-4 garlic gloves, minced

1 ½ pounds of chicken- cooked and shredded

9 cups of chicken broth

1- 8-ounce package of your favorite fresh refrigerated tortellini

¼ cup heavy cream

1 cup baby spinach, roughly chopped

2 tablespoons chopped parsley

1 teaspoons fresh thyme

½ teaspoon of crushed red pepper

Salt and Pepper to taste

Directions:

In a large pot on medium heat, add the olive oil and chopped carrots, cook for a couple of minutes, add onions and bell pepper, cook for a couple more minutes. Add garlic and cook for another two minutes. Add chicken broth, chicken, crushed red pepper and salt and pepper to taste. Bring to a boil and simmer for about 15 minutes. Bring back to a boil and add the tortellini and cook for 5-7 minutes. Stir in the heavy cream. Add spinach and fresh herbs. Serve with garlic bread.

Tortilla Soup

This is a soup you can modify in all kinds of ways to make it to your liking. I just love a basic tortilla soup topped with lots of melted cheese and chopped avocado.

Ingredients:

1 diced onion

2 cloves of fresh garlic, minced

1 teaspoon paprika

2 teaspoons chili powder

3 teaspoons cumin

64 ounces of chicken broth

1 – 14 ounce can of diced fire roasted tomatoes

1 whole cooked chicken, shredded

1 tablespoon olive oil

Salt and pepper to taste

Optional toppings:

Tortilla chips or strips

Chopped green onion

Shredded cheese, I like Colby Jack

Chopped avocado

Directions:

In a large stock pot over medium heat add 1 tablespoon of olive oil. Sauté onions until translucent, add garlic and cook for two minutes. Stir in spices. Add chicken stock and tomatoes. Bring to a boil and simmer for 15 minutes. Add chicken and simmer for 15 more minutes. Serve in bowls with whichever toppings you like.

Green Chili Pozole

If you have ever had Pozole you know that it's usually in a red type sauce. I do like that version of Pozole, however I like this lighter version much better. It's like a Mexican chili that can be topped with so many things to add to its deliciousness. You can use shredded pork or chicken, either is delicious. I will often cook a whole chicken cooked the day before or use rotisserie. If using pork, I will cook a roast in the crock pot the day before.

Ingredients:

2-4 cups cooked shredded pork or chicken

24 ounces chicken broth

2-8 ounce cans hominy, drained and rinsed

8 ounces chopped green chilies

½ diced onion

2-3 fresh garlic cloves, minced

1 tablespoon olive oil

1 tablespoon of cumin

1 teaspoon of Mexican oregano

Salt and Pepper to taste

Optional Toppings:

Shredded Monterey Jack Cheese

Chopped Avocado

Chopped Cilantro

Lime wedges

Directions:

In a stock pot over medium heat add oil and onions and sauté until transparent. Add minced garlic and good for 2 minutes. Add in the broth and the rest of the ingredients (minus the toppings). Simmer for at least 30 minutes. Serve in a soup bowl and serve with your favorite optional toppings. Add the juice from the lime wedge right before eating brings such a freshness to this dish.

Kim Richardson

Inspiration

MAIN DISHES

The main attraction is here! Many of these dishes could be served as lunch or dinner. They can be a one dish meal or get creative with a fun salad for a side.

Chicken Pot Pie

Pot Pies are the ultimate comfort food for me. I love a creamy sauce and a crispy flaky crust. You can use chicken or if you are looking for a vegetarian option just omit it and add your favorite veggies. You can also make a large one or several small ones.

Ingredients:

½ cup butter

½ cup chopped/mined celery

½ cup chopped/mined carrot

½ cup chopped/minced onion

3 garlic gloves minced

1 whole cooked chicken- meat removed and shredded

4 tablespoons flour

2- 15-ounce cans of chicken broth

⅔ cup of milk or heavy cream

1 scrambled egg

Salt/pepper to taste

Pre-made refrigerated pie crust, or you could make homemade pie crust on page 168

Directions:

Pre-heat oven to 425 degrees. Place one of the pie crust in a baking dish and prick the bottom with a fork several times. Bake for 5-6 mins. In a large pan melt butter, add in onion, carrot, and celery and cook until onions are transparent. Stir in garlic and cook for an additional couple of minutes. Add salt and pepper. Add flour and cook for a couple of minutes. Add in chicken broth constantly stirring to ensure you will not get lumps. Add milk or cream. Stir in the chicken.

Add chicken mixture into pre-baked pie crust. Top with the other crust, seal the edges. Poke several holes in the top to let steam escape. Wrap the edges of the pie crust with foil or use a pie protector. Bake for 25 minutes, remove foil. Brush the scrambled egg wash over the top of the crust and bake another 10-15 minutes until nicely browned. Let cool for 10 minutes before serving.

Flat Bread Pizza

This can make a great little lunch or dinner and, in our house, I will make all the flat bread crusts and have various toppings for everyone to create their own favorite pizza.

Ingredients:

4 cups flour

1 teaspoon salt

1 ½ ounces butter

1 ½ cups milk

Olive oil- seasonings

Directions:

Melt butter and milk together. Mix all ingredients – wrap and let sit at room temperature for 30 minutes. Optional- mix herbs in with bread- garlic, rosemary

Cook- one of two ways

1. Heat Olive oil in pan and heat each side for a couple of minutes

2. Heat grill- brush oil (can add herbs to oil) and grill each side for a couple of minutes

Once the crust is complete you can add your favorite toppings- sauce, cheese, meat, and/or veggies. Bake for about 10 minutes until cheese is melted and bubbly.

Honey Mustard Chicken

Sometimes people just want meat and bacon seems to make everything taste better. It is a super simple recipe that can be served with rice or just a side of your favorite vegetables.

Ingredients:

4 chicken breasts
¾ cup honey
½ cup mustard
Lemon pepper to taste
4 slices bacon
1 cup Mozzarella cheese

Directions:

Heat oven to 375 degrees. Place chicken in casserole dish. Drizzle honey, mustard and lemon pepper. Bake for 25 minutes. Top with 2 bacon slice halves and cheese. Bake another 10 min

Portobello Mushroom Burgers

These are a great alternative to beef burgers. This is different than most; it's chopped fine and will be somewhat crumbly in texture like a beef burger. Everyone loves this recipe, even those who do not like mushrooms or really love beef burgers and are skeptical of veggie burgers.

Ingredients:

2 cups Portabella mushrooms- chopped fine

1 cup cooked black beans, rinsed or purchased refried black beans to save some time.

1 cup minced broccoli- finely chopped

½ cup red onion

1 egg beaten

1-2 cups panko crumbs or gluten free bread crumbs

1 tablespoon Montreal steak seasoning

1 tablespoon Worcestershire sauce

2 tablespoon minced garlic

¾ cup fresh Parmesan

Olive Oil

Directions:

Heat skillet on medium heat. In a large bowl add 1 cup mashes (or refried) beans. This is where I wear gloves and just get my hands in there; add mushrooms, broccoli, garlic, onion, Worcestershire and steak seasoning and mix thoroughly. Add in egg and bread crumbs, you may need to add more bread crumbs as you want your mixture more dry and crumbly than wet. Form into patties. This makes quite a bit so if you have 2-4 people consider halving this recipe.

Add oil to pan, once it simmers add your formed patty 3-4 min each side. Serve with your favorite toppings. My favorite is provolone cheese, pesto mayo and avocado.

Cilantro Chicken

This chicken can be grilled or baked, either way it's delicious. I love cooking up large batches that I can use the chicken in my salads throughout the week. You could serve it with some Spanish rice or Quinoa and it will be a hit that is super healthy too.

Ingredients:

¼ cup lime juice
½ cup cilantro
½ teaspoon minced garlic
1 tablespoon honey
1 tablespoon oil
½ cup white wine or rice wine vinegar
Salt/pepper
4- chicken breast

Directions:

Mix marinade in a sealable bag. Place chicken breast in marinade for at least a few hours, overnight is best. You can either grill these or bake them in the oven. If you are baking in the oven, usually 400 degrees for about 20-25 minutes is perfect.

Chicken and Mushrooms

If you are like me and love mushrooms and love cheese you will love this recipe. I like to serve this with some garlic mashed potatoes on the side.

Ingredients:

3 cups sliced mushrooms

4 chicken breasts

2 eggs scrambled

1 cup bread crumbs

2 tablespoons butter

6 ounces shredded Mozzarella cheese

¾ cup broth

Directions:

Heat oven 350 degrees. Place ½ mushrooms in casserole dish. Dip chicken into eggs then bread crumbs and brown in a medium heat skillet for a few minutes on each side until nicely browned. Place chicken in casserole top with mushrooms and cheese. Add broth to dish. Bake 30-35 min until chicken is no longer pink.

Beef Tacos

Place a chuck roast in the crockpot. Sprinkle with cumin, garlic seasoning and top with a can of Rotel. Cook on low for 8 hrs. Shred and remove fat. Serve with your favorite tortillas and taco fixings.

Enchiladas

I used to buy canned sauce until I learned how much sodium it had. I decided to try to make my own and once I did I never looked back because of course the homemade version was so much better and it's not hard to do! When cooking for a variety of people I will use vegetable broth instead of chicken broth so that it meets everyone's needs.

Enchilada Sauces:
Red Sauce
Ingredients:

6 Tomatoes

3 Jalapenos

1 small onion

3-6 garlic cloves

3 guajillo dehydrated red chilies

1 can chicken broth or vegetable broth for vegan option

1 teaspoon oregano

Salt/pepper to taste

Directions:

Preheat oven 400 degrees. Toast guajillo chilies on a hot skillet for a few minutes each side then place in cold water to soak. Line a baking dish in foil, you will thank me later when cleanup is easy! Cut tomatoes and onions into quarters. Peel 3-6 garlic cloves, I love garlic and believe you can never have too much; use the amount you would like. I usually use 4-5 of the largest pieces. Remove stems and cut jalapenos in half. I like to remove the insides with the seeds to help make this sauce a little bit milder, made this way the sauce is about medium in spice. If you like it spicy leave the seeds in, less spicy use only 1 jalapeno with seeds removed. Place tomatoes, onion, jalapeno, and garlic in your foil lined pan. Sprinkle with salt and pepper and place in the oven until mixture is soft, about 45 mins. Remove mixture from the oven and let cool at least 30-40 mins.

Remove guajillo chilies from the water and remove stems (again if you like it less spicy then be sure to remove the seeds as well. Place chilies and roasted veggie mixture into blender with a little bit of Olive Oil and cilantro. If you want the sauce thinner, you can use a little (chicken or vegetable) broth to the blender. Mix until creamy. Place in refrigerator until ready for use, many times I make the sauce in the morning or even the day before. Place the sauce in a pan to heat right before you are ready to use.

Green Sauce

Ingredients:

4 tomatillos

2 large green chilies

½ bunch of cilantro

2 cloves of garlic

½ onion

1-2 jalapenos (depending on the heat desired)

1 can chicken broth or vegetable broth for vegan option

Salt and Pepper to taste

Olive Oil

Directions:

Preheat oven 400 degrees. Line a baking dish in foil, you will thank me later when cleanup is easy! Cut tomatillos and onions into quarters. Peel garlic cloves, I love garlic and believe you can never have too much; use the amount you would like. Remove stems and cut jalapenos in half. I like to remove the insides with the seeds to help make this sauce a little bit milder, made this way the sauce is about medium in spice. If you like it spicy leave the seeds in, less spicy use only 1 jalapeno with seeds removed. Place tomatillos, onion, jalapeno, and garlic in your foil lined pan. Sprinkle with salt and pepper and place in the oven until mixture is soft, about 45 mins. Remove mixture from the oven and let cool at least 30-40 mins.

Place roasted veggie mixture into blender. Add 1 can of broth and oregano to the blender. Mix until creamy. Place in refrigerator until ready for use, many times I make the sauce in the morning or even the day before. Place the sauce in a pan to heat right before you are ready to use.

Enchilada Fillings

Meat- If I am using the crockpot I usually will cook the meat the day before. We might have tacos and then use the leftovers for enchiladas.

Beef- Chuck Roast in the crock pot (7-8hrs), sprinkle with salt, cumin, and garlic seasoning- shred when ready to use.

Chicken- 4 chicken breast (6-7 hours on low) in the crock pot with a can of Rotel, add some cumin and garlic seasoning. Sometimes, I will cook a whole chicken in the oven the day before or if I want to save time I will buy a pre-cooked rotisserie chicken.

Cheese of your choice- I usually use Colby/Jack.

Vegetarian- Use cheese of your choice and veggie mixture (see vegan mixture below)

Vegan- create a veggie mixture of choice; yellow squash, zucchini, mushrooms, onions, and potatoes work great as a filling for enchiladas.

Fresh Cilantro chopped fine

Corn tortillas- I use the ones that are in the refrigerator section the grocery store. You cook them right before you use them. These tortillas taste so much better, they are larger, they don't break, and you don't have to soak them in oil. They are so worth it!!

Directions:

Preheat oven to 350 degrees. Heat sauce in saucepan just to warm. Cook tortillas on a hot skillet. This takes a little bit of time; however, you are skipping the old way of cooking them in oil which would take the same amount of time.

Spray your baking dish with non-stick cooking spray. Spread a thin layer of sauce on the bottom of your baking dish. I like to mix a little bit of the sauce in with my filling mixture for flavor. Fill your corn tortillas with filling of choice (add cheese if desired) and place in baking dish. Spread sauce over the top of the enchiladas, Sprinkle with cheese if desired. Bake for 30 mins. As soon as you pull the enchiladas out of the oven sprinkle with cilantro and let cool 5-10 mins before serving.

French Dip Sandwiches

So easy and so delicious! This is another one I like to make the day before just because I like to refrigerate the au jus` so the fat hardens to the top and can be removed easily. It just makes for a better less greasy sauce. You can save the leftover broth to make gravy, add in a soup, or freeze it for later.

Place ingredients in slow cooker:

Chuck Roast

2 tablespoons soy sauce

1 bf bouillon cube

1 bay leaf

¼ teaspoon Black pepper

1 teaspoon dried thyme

1 teaspoon garlic powder

1 cup water

Directions:

Cover and cook on low for 7-8 hours. Let cool, spoon broth over roast to keep moist

While roast is cooling, using a ladle remove most of the broth into a bowl.

I like to refrigerate the broth for a while. The fat will separate and placing it in the fridge allows the fat to become solid on the top. After fat is solid spoon it out and add water to taste for aus ju`. Heat just before serving.

Use which ever toppings you enjoy such as:
Sautéed Mushrooms
Sautéed Onions
Sautéed Peppers
Cheese, I prefer provolone

Use whichever bread you enjoy for sandwiches:
Sub rolls
Hamburger buns
Slider buns
Texas Toast

We like to make our sandwiches and place in the oven 350 degrees for a few minutes to melt the cheese and slightly toast the bread.

If you have left-over beef you can make beef and gravy with potatoes, quesadillas, or tacos. Don't be afraid to get creative!

Chicken Lettuce Wraps

I have tried many recipes, and this is one that is closest to a copycat recipe for PF Chang's Chicken Lettuce Wraps. I like them just this way with a little bit of the special sauce to add a little heat. However, feel free to add a variety of toppings such as, julienned carrots, julienned peppers, bean sprouts, cilantro, or chopped nuts.

Ingredients:

4 tablespoons sesame oil

1-pound ground chicken

1- 8 ounce can water chestnuts

1 package mushrooms finely chopped

2 green onions chopped

3 tablespoons soy sauce

½ tablespoon mirin

2 tablespoons oyster sauce

1 tablespoon rice vinegar

Special Sauce
Ingredients:

¼ cup sugar

½ cup water

2 tablespoons soy sauce

2 tablespoons rice wine vinegar

2 tablespoons ketchup

1 tablespoon lemon juice

½ teaspoon sesame oil

1 tablespoon hot mustard

1-2 teaspoons chili paste

Optional: add some chopped green onions and freshly grated ginger

Directions:

In a large skillet add 2 tablespoons of oils and brown chicken. I like to go one step further and place the cooked chicken in the food processor and pulse just a few times to have a minced chicken mixture. Add oil- sauté water chestnuts, mushrooms and scallions. Add chicken with soy sauce, mirin, oyster sauce and rice vinegar. Mix all ingredients for the special sauce in a separate bowl. Serve in lettuce cups with desired toppings and special sauce.

Vegan Lettuce Wraps

I have tried many recipes, and this is one that is closest to a copycat recipe for PF Chang's Veggie Lettuce Wraps. I like them just this way with a little bit of the special sauce to add a little heat. However, feel free to add a variety of toppings such as, julienned carrots, julienned peppers, bean sprouts, cilantro, or chopped nuts.

Ingredients:

3 tablespoons hoisin sauce

3 tablespoons reduced-sodium soy sauce

2 tablespoons rice vinegar

1 teaspoon sesame oil

2 teaspoons olive oil

1 (12- to 14-ounce) package extra-firm tofu (do not use silken)

8 ounces baby bella (cremini) mushrooms, finely chopped

1 (8-ounce) can water chestnuts, drained and finely chopped

2 cloves garlic, minced

2 teaspoons freshly grated ginger

¼ teaspoon red pepper flakes (omit if sensitive to spice)

4 green onions, thinly sliced, divided

Special Sauce

Ingredients:

¼ cup sugar

½ cup water

2 tablespoons soy sauce

2 tablespoons rice wine vinegar

2 tablespoons ketchup

1 tablespoon lemon juice

½ teaspoon sesame oil

1 tablespoon hot mustard

1-2 teaspoons chili paste

Optional: add some chopped green onions and freshly grated ginger

Directions:

In a small bowl, stir together the hoisin, soy sauce, rice vinegar, and sesame oil. Set aside.

Press the tofu between paper towels to squeeze out as much liquid as possible. Refresh the paper towels and press again. Heat the 2 teaspoons olive oil in a large nonstick skillet over medium-high. Once the oil is hot, crumble in the tofu, breaking it into very small pieces as it cooks. Continue cooking for 5 minutes, then add the diced mushrooms. Continue cooking until any remaining tofu liquid cooks off and the tofu starts to turn golden, about 3 minutes more. Stir in the water chestnuts, garlic, ginger, red pepper flakes, and half of the green onions and cook until fragrant, about 30 seconds more.

Pour the sauce over the top of the tofu mixture and stir to coat. Cook just until you hear bubbling and the sauce is warmed through, 30 to 60 seconds. Mix all ingredients for the special sauce in a separate bowl.

Spoon the tofu mixture into individual lettuce leaves. Top with remaining green onions, grated carrots, and additional red pepper flakes as desired. Enjoy immediately. Serve in lettuce cups with desired toppings and special sauce. The tofu filling can be refrigerated for 3 to 5 days. Reheat gently with a bit of water or stock to prevent it from drying out or in a skillet over medium heat. Try the leftovers mixed with rice or scrambled with eggs.

Inspiration

Chicken in Lemon Sauce

This is my version of chicken piccata. It goes well with pasta of your choice or zoodles (zucchini noodles) or any pasta.

Ingredients:

4 Chicken Breasts

1 (14 ounce) can of broth

½ onion chopped fine

1 teaspoon garlic seasoning

1 tablespoon butter

1 teaspoon olive oil

1 teaspoon cornstarch

¼ cup white wine

Salt/Pepper to taste

Optional – ¼ pound of prosciutto chopped fine and fried.

Optional Zoodles: zucchini and/or yellow squash

Directions:

Pre-heat oven to 400 degrees. Place the olive oil into pan on medium heat. Place chicken breast in the pan and season with garlic seasoning, salt and pepper. Brown the chicken on both sides. Once the Chicken is browned on both sides place the chicken in the oven to finish cooking. Add a little drop of olive oil to your pan and sauté` the onion until transparent set aside. Add wine to the pan and boil for a couple of minutes to burn off the alcohol. Add the chicken broth to the pan. Season with salt, pepper, and garlic seasoning. Mix the cornstarch with a little broth or water and whisk mixture into the sauce to thicken. Add chicken to sauce and simmer for a couple of minutes.

You can prepare your favorite pasta or zoodles for a side. When plating, place the chicken and sauce over the noodles and sprinkle a little friend prosciutto over the top if desired. Additional add in options- Sautéed mushrooms, zucchini, or yellow squash go great with this as well.

Zoodles: Use a spiralizer to spiral cut your squash. Line a cookie sheet with foil or parchment paper. Place your zoodles on the cookie sheet, sprinkle lightly with salt and pepper. Bake at about 250 degrees until slightly soft. I like mine to have a little crunch and not to be soggy. These cook quickly so keep an eye on them.

Caprese Stuffed Portobello Mushrooms

These are so delicious! They can be served as the main dish or a side dish.

Ingredients:

4-6 large Portobello mushrooms

1 package of grape or cherry tomatoes

6-8 basil leaves, chopped or sliced thin

Fresh Mozzarella cheese, sliced or cut into small 1-inch pieces

¼ cup balsamic vinegar

2 cloves of garlic

2 tablespoons of butter

Olive oil

Directions:

Place the vinegar in a small sauce pan and bring to a boil and let reduce. Stay close by and stir often as it can burn quickly. You will know when it has reduced enough when it coats a spoon. Using a spoon, clean the gills of the mushrooms and discard. Melt the butter and mix with garlic cloves. Completely dry the mushrooms. Brush the mushrooms with garlic/butter mixture. Slice the tomatoes in half. Place tomatoes and basil inside the mushrooms.

Top with Mozzarella cheese and sprinkle with more

basil. You can cook these on the grill or in the oven. Cook about 400 degrees until cheese is bubbly and slightly browned. Drizzle your balsamic glaze over the top.

Veggie Lasagna

This is a versatile dish and can be customized in so many ways with a variety of cheeses and vegetables. Every time I make it it's different depending on what vegetables are in season and what I have on hand. Here is my basic recipe, feel free to get creative and make it to your liking.

Ingredients:

2 jars of your favorite Spaghetti Sauce

1 package lasagna noodles

1 large block of Mozzarella cheese, shredded.

2 Zucchini- sliced thin

2 Yellow Squash- sliced thin

1 packaged mushrooms- cleaned and sliced

Basil – chopped fine

Oregano- chopped fine

Freshly Grated Parmesan cheese

Directions:

Cook, rinse and cool the lasagna noodles. Preheat oven 350 degrees. Spray a baking dish with non-stick spray or coat with olive oil. Place a little bit of sauce in the bottom of the pan. Place a layer of noodles, more sauce, top with layers of vegetables, then Mozzarella cheese. Sprinkle with chopped herbs. Layer again, noodles, sauce, veggies and cheese. Continue layering until pan is full. Be sure to end with Mozzarella cheese on the top and sprinkle some fresh grated Parmesan on the top. If you really like Parmesan, then add it to each layer. Bake for about 30 minutes or until cheese is bubbly and slightly browned.

Kim Richardson

Inspiration

DESSERTS

Oh, how I love dessert! I do not make dessert often, usually for guest or special occasions, so they really seem like a treat. I enjoy using heart shape molds in many of these recipes to create that high vibe feeling when eating.

Apple Galette`

I love making this version of apple pie. It has a rustic look, so you do not have to worry about having the prettiest pie and it's oh so delicious! You can make one large one or small individual ones, either way it's sure to be a hit. You can make your own pie crust or purchase one ready-made. If you purchase one ready-made, then roll it out to thin it and make it a little bit larger.

Serve with vanilla ice cream. If you have left over filling it goes great on ice cream too!

Ingredients:

Pie Crust:

1 ½ cups all-purpose flour

1 ½ teaspoons sugar

¼ teaspoon salt

1 stick (1/2 cup) plus 2 tablespoons cold unsalted butter

⅓ cup water

Galette`:

4 Golden Delicious apples

2 tablespoons sugar

½ teaspoon cinnamon

1 tablespoon unsalted butter cut into small pieces

3 tablespoons of apricot preserves

2 tablespoons of milk

Optional: You can add your favorite chopped nuts

Directions:

In a food processor, combine flour with sugar, salt and butter and process for about 5 seconds. Sprinkle with ice water over the flour mixture and process until the pastry just begins to come together, about ten seconds; you should still see small amounts of butter in it. Transfer the pastry to a work surface, bring together to form a ball and place in plastic wrap then place in the fridge until chilled.

Preheat oven to 400 degrees. Peel and core the apples and chop them into small bite site pieces. In a small bowl combine sugar and cinnamon and stir in the apples.

Remove pie crust from the fridge and roll out into a thin circle, place on a baking sheet lined with parchment paper. Spread the apples over the pastry leaving about 1 inch from the edges. Chop the tablespoon of butter into small pieces and sprinkle over the apples. Fold up the sides over the apples. Brush the crust with milk. Bake for about 45 minutes until apples are bubbly and crust is browned. While the dessert is in the oven, heat the apricot preserves in a small pan with a drizzle of water to thin a bit. Once the galette` comes out of the oven brush the top with the glaze and if you like nuts sprinkle them on now. Serve warm with ice cream.

Not So Fried Ice Cream

This dessert is always a big hit! It can be served anytime, however it's my go to dessert on Mexican night.

Ingredients:

1 cup cornflake crumbs

⅓ cup sugar

⅓ cup butter, melted

¾ teaspoon ground cinnamon

½ gallon butter pecan ice cream, softened, divided

4 tablespoons honey, divided

Directions:

In a small bowl, combine the cornflake crumbs, sugar, butter and cinnamon; set aside 1/2 cup. Press remaining crumb mixture into a greased 9-in. springform pan. Spoon half of the ice cream over crust. Sprinkle with reserved crumb mixture; drizzle with 2 tablespoons honey. Cover and freeze for 2 hours.

Top with remaining ice cream. Cover and freeze for 8 hours or overnight.

Remove from the freezer 5 minutes before serving. Remove sides of pan; drizzle with remaining honey.

Pineapple Whip

This is a dairy free, healthy alternative to the "Dole Whip" that is loaded with sugar. This can be served as a dessert or a breakfast smoothie. I have also been known to mix in my favorite clear alcohol (Malibu Rum, White Rum or Vodka) for a tasty after dinner drink. This whip is so easy to make with the right blender!

Ingredients:

1 pineapples- Cut up and frozen
1 cup coconut milk

Directions:

I usually cut the pineapple the day before I plan on making it, so it will be frozen. About 30 mins before I plan on making this whip I will pull the pineapple out of the freezer to soften it just a little bit.

Add the slightly thawed pineapple and coconut milk to your blender, mix well and serve immediately.

Dairy Free Chocolate Mousse

This is a great dairy free alternative to traditional chocolate mousse. I like to use the mousse to fill chocolate cups (made with fun shaped silicone molds and melted chocolate) and top with fruit such as strawberries, raspberries, and black berries (see picture at the end of this book). This is also a great substitute for chocolate icing too!

Ingredients:

40 gr or 2 squares 70% chocolate Bar

6 tablespoons Cocoa Powder- unsweetened

2 pinches of salt

4- 400ml (13.7 ounces) cans full fat coconut cream

4 tablespoons of powdered sugar

Directions:

Refrigerate coconut Cream overnight, in a large bowl scoop out cream discard liquid. Add sugar and using an electric mixture beat on high until foamy. Fold in cocoa powder and salt. Grate the chocolate bar into the mixture. Refrigerate until chilled and ready to serve.

Chocolate Whip Cream

I will use this on muffins, cakes, pies and cookies. It's a great filling for cupcakes too. This is delicious served with a variety of fruit as well. Try topping your hot cocoa too!

Ingredients:

2 cups heavy cream
¼ cup cocoa powder
½ cup powdered sugar

Directions:

Place a metal mixing bowl and beaters in the freezer for 15 minutes. Remove the bowl from the freezer. Add the heavy cream, cocoa powder, and powdered sugar, and beat with an electric mixer for 4-5 minutes, or until stiff peaks form, it's scoop-able with a spoon and holds its shape.

Use on cakes, cupcakes, pies, hot cocoa, etc. Place leftovers in a container and store in the fridge.

Kim Richardson

Inspiration

No Churn Lemon Ice Cream

Even ice cream is loaded with all kinds of unnecessary ingredients. One night I was craving some ice cream and I do not have anything to churn the ice cream, I had to find a recipe that would work with what I had. I came up with this and let me tell you it's very delicious. Once frozen it does become a lot harder than normal ice cream, no worries though! Just let it sit out of the freezer for 5-10 minutes and it will be the perfect consistency for serving.

Ingredients:

1 teaspoon lemon jest
2 teaspoon fresh lemon juice
1 teaspoon vanilla extract
1- 14 ounces can condensed milk, sweetened
2 cups heavy cream

Directions:

Place all ingredients in a mixing bowl and mix on high until soft peaks form. Place in an airtight container and freeze.

Strawberry Lemonade Cheesecake

Personally, I am not a fan of cheesecake. It has been difficult for me to find one that I can enjoy. This is the first cheesecake I have truly loved! It's an easy no bake recipe, can be made ahead, and it is always a big hit whenever I serve it! Someone said that this was better than The Cheesecake Factory, what a compliment!

Ingredients:

For the crust:

1 sleeve (9 crackers, 140 grams) graham crackers

4 tablespoons (57 grams) unsalted butter, melted

For the cheesecake:

12 ounces (340 grams) cream cheese, at room temperature

½ cup (100 grams) granulated sugar

¾ cup (180 grams) heavy cream

Zest of 1 lemon

¼ cup lemon juice

For topping:

5 ounces (142 grams) strawberries, hulled and chopped

1 tablespoon granulated sugar

2 teaspoons lemon juice

Strawberry slices

Lemon slices

Directions:

For the crust:

Thoroughly grease a mini cheesecake pan (I use a muffin pan). Place the graham crackers in the bowl of a food processor and pulse until finely ground. Add in the melted butter and pulse until moistened. Divide the mixture among the cavities of the cheesecake pan, about 1 heaping tablespoon in each. Firmly press into the bottom of each cavity (a shot glass or other small object makes easy work of this). Set aside.

For the cheesecake:

In the bowl of an electric mixer, beat the cream cheese and sugar on medium-high speed until creamy and well combined. Add in the cream, zest, and juice and continue beating until well combined and thickened. Divide the mixture among each cavity and cover with plastic wrap.

Chill until firm, at least 4 hours or overnight. The cheesecake can be stored in the fridge in an airtight container for up to 2 days.

For the topping:

Combine the strawberries, sugar, and lemon juice in the bowl of a blender or food processor and pulse until pureed. Top each cheesecake with a dollop of the sauce.

Garnish with a strawberry and lemon slice and serve.

I will usually make the cheesecakes and the sauce the day before. Do not place the strawberry topping on the cheesecake until you are ready to serve.

Spinach Ice Cream

This is a recipe that came with my BlendTec blender and you wouldn't believe how much the kids love this!

Ingredients:

¾ cup half and half

¼ cup agave

½ banana

⅔ cup nonfat dry milk

2 cup spinach, lightly packed

1 ½ tablespoons vanilla extract

2 ½ - 3 cups ice cubes

Directions:

Add ingredients to blender, blend well. Serve right away. If there are any leftovers you can freeze but you will need to thaw a few minutes to get a softer texture for serving.

Strawberry Shortcake Kabobs

These are fun and look so fancy at any get together.

Ingredients:

½ cup butter, softened

1 cup sugar

2 eggs

1 teaspoon baking powder

¼ teaspoon salt

1 ½ cup flour

¾ milk

1 teaspoon vanilla extract

Strawberries

Vanilla candy coating

Skewers

Directions:

Preheat oven 350 degrees. In a large bowl, beat sugar and butter until creamy. Mix in eggs, baking powder and salt. Alternate between adding flour and milk, beating until all ingredients are combined. Stir in vanilla. Use a larger cake pan (11x16) to bake this cake so the when you cut in into squares the squares won't be too large. Pour batter into a greased and floured (or use parchment paper for easy clean up), bake for 18-20 minutes until toothpick comes out clean. Let cake cool and cut in 1-inch squares.

Rinse and cut off tops to strawberries. Place strawberry on the skewer (it will stay in place better is the strawberry is on the bottom). Then place a square of cake then strawberry them cake then strawberry. Place the skewers in a parchment paper lined baking sheet. Melt the white candy coating/white chocolate and drizzle over the skewers. Refrigerate at least 30 mins before serving.

Strawberry Shortcake Bars

Who doesn't love strawberry shortcake!

Ingredients:
Cake:

½ cup butter, softened

1 cup sugar

2 eggs

1 teaspoon baking powder

¼ teaspoon salt

1 ½ cup flour

¾ milk

1 teaspoon vanilla extract

1-pint strawberries

Frosting:

8 ounces cream cheese, softened

¼ cup powdered sugar

8 ounces frozen whipped topping

Directions:

Preheat oven 350 degrees. In a large bowl, beat sugar and butter until creamy. Mix in eggs, baking powder and salt. Alternate between adding flour and milk, beating until all ingredients are combined. Stir in vanilla. Pour batter into a greased and floured (or use parchment paper for easy clean up), bake for 18-20 minutes until toothpick comes out clean. Dice up strawberries and set aside. In a large bowl combine cream cheese, powered sugar and frozen whipped topping. Spread over cooled cake and top with strawberries. Refrigerate for at least 3 hours before serving.

No Bake Chocolate Tart

This tasty recipe is vegan and gluten free. This is a no bake recipe that has two parts to it; the crust and the filling.

Ingredients:
The crust:

½ cup pitted Medjool dates

1 cups almonds

1 ounces 70% dark chocolate

1 tablespoon coconut oil

Pinch of salt

The filling:

1 cup coconut cream

3 ½ ounces of 70% dark chocolate

¼ cup coconut oil

½ cup pitted Medjool dates

1 teaspoon vanilla extract

Directions:

If the dates are not soft already, soak them in water for 10 minutes. Add dates to food processors and pulse until fine. Add melted chocolate, coconut oil, and salt. Pulse until mix thoroughly.

Press the crust into a round tart pan (or make mini tarts using silicone cupcake molds). Chill until set.

Heat coconut cream, chocolate and coconut oil until melted. Place the dates in the food processor and add the melted mixture and vanilla. Pulse until smooth and combined. Pour the filling into the tart pan. Refrigerate at least two hours before serving.

Topping ideas; whipped coconut cream, sliced almonds, various fruit- strawberries, raspberries, or blackberries.

Brownies

I love brownies! I wanted to get away from the pre-packed box version, so I came up with this recipe. I love that this only makes 6-8 brownies, the perfect amount for our family. I have made dry batches of this and gave them as gifts. If you want to create your own ready to go brownie mix for later or want to give them as gifts; mix the dry ingredients together and label with the wet ingredients to add and the baking instructions.

Ingredients:

1 cup white sugar

⅓ cup unsweetened cocoa powder

½ cup flour

¼ teaspoon salt

¼ teaspoon baking powder

½ cup melted butter

2 eggs

1 teaspoon vanilla

Directions:

Pre-heat oven to 350 degrees. Using a whisk or flour shifter, mix all dry ingredients together. Melt butter set aside and let cool. In a large bowl beat the eggs, butter, and vanilla together. Stir in dry ingredients. Spread batter into a small square pan, you can line the pan with parchment paper sprayed with oil for easy clean up. Bake for 22-35 minutes depending on your preference. Use a knife to check for doneness. I like my brownies more like cake, so I cook them a bit longer. If you like them gooey then cook them less.

Optional add ins before baking:

Chopped Nuts

Chocolate Chips

Chopped Andi's chocolate mint candies

I love to add drops of peanut butter and swirls around with a toothpick

Optional- Frost the top with chocolate, peanut butter frosting, or you can place some Andi's chocolate mint candies right on top just as you pull the brownies out of the oven.

Kim Richardson

Inspiration

Chocolate Heart Shaped Cups filled with Dairy Free Chocolate Mousse and Berries

Plants seeds of love everywhere you go.

I would love to hear about your journey with food and how eating in a high vibrational way has changed your life, feel free to send me an email at kim.richardson@kimrichardson.kim or to receive more inspiration, recipes, and to be in the know of current events and sales, sign up for my newsletter on my website at www.kimrichardson.kim

Kim Richardson ♡
www.kimrichardson.kim

ABOUT THE AUTHOR

Kim Richardson is an author, teacher, motivational speaker, coach, mentor, ordained minister, and certified Mind Body Spirit Practitioner. Through sharing her own personal experiences, she empowers individuals to transform their lives. She helps individuals to heal, forgive and expand without judgement. Her passion is helping people discover their true gifts and how to use them in the world. Kim teaches with unconditional love as she hopes it will have a ripple effect in the world.

Kim has a love and passion for food. She loves creating high vibrational dishes and uses this passion to cook for others in her catering business.

Kim resides in Payson, Arizona where she enjoys the warm weather and sunshine with her fiancé', Symon and their two fur babies, Hudson and Casey.

To learn more about Kim's work visit
www.kimrichardson.kim

Connect with Kim on Facebook:
www.facebook.com/kimrichardson444

Additional Books Available by Kim Richardson

Living Your Purpose

Spiritual Leaders Top Picks

365 Days of Angel Prayers

Resources:

The Paleo Approach by Sarah Ballantyne and Robb Wolf

The Whole 30 by Melissa and Dallas Hartwig

Printed in Great Britain
by Amazon